Grow a Dazzling Divinatory
Tool in Your Own Garden

The greatest gift divination can grant you is an insight into your life that you would not otherwise attain. A divinatory system such as the Victorian flower oracle is a powerful tool for helping you cope with daily experiences, bringing you a refreshed perspective to effect creative, positive solutions to problems and a new outlook on current issues in your life.

The Victorian Flower Oracle describes an easy process for creating a completely unique and personalized form of divination for yourself—a system that will work beautifully for you regardless of your level of experience since you create your very own deck out of pressed flowers, decoupage, wood, or stone. After you have created your magical oracle and have experimented with the fascinating interpretive layouts, this charming book will continue to give you hours of pleasure with a veritable treasury of the attributes of more than seventy flowers, herbs, and trees—information that you can use to make a variety of health and beauty aids, foods, beverages, and gifts.

The tradition of ascribing symbolism to natural surroundings is a very old one. If you see nature as a reflection of divinity, then this book will show you how understanding the language of flowers can open up new channels for communicating with the divine spark in nature … to truly enhance your daily magical living!

About the Author

Patricia Telesco is an ordained minister with the Universal Life Church and a professional member of the Wiccan-Pagan Press Alliance. Her hobbies include Celtic illumination, playing harp and dulcimer, historical costuming, writing and singing folk music, sufi dancing, historical herbalism studies, carving wood and soapstone, poetry, and the Society for Creative Anachronism (a historical re-creation group). Many of these activities have extended themselves into her small mail-order business called Hourglass Creations. Her articles and poems have appeared in journals such as *Circle*, *The Unicorn*, *Moonstone* (England), *Demeter's Emerald*, *Silver Chalice*, and *Llewellyn's New Worlds of Mind and Spirit* (formerly *New Times*). She is also the author of *A Victorian Grimoire*, *The Urban Pagan*, and *Llewellyn's 1994 Magical Almanac*. She welcomes the opportunity to do workshops and lectures. Patricia lives in Buffalo, New York, with her husband, son, dog, and six cats.

To Write to the Author

If you wish to contact the author or would like more information about this book, please write to the author in care of Llewellyn Worldwide, and we will forward your request. Both the author and publisher appreciate hearing from you and learning of your enjoyment of this book and how it has helped you. Llewellyn Worldwide cannot guarantee that every letter written to the author can be answered, but all will be forwarded. Please write to:

Patricia Telesco
c/o Llewellyn Worldwide
P.O. Box 64383-786, St. Paul, MN 55164-0383, U.S.A.

Please enclose a self-addressed, stamped envelope for reply, or $1.00 to cover costs.
If outside the U.S.A., enclose international postal reply coupon.

Free Catalog from Llewellyn

For more than ninety years Llewellyn has brought its readers knowledge in the fields of metaphysics and human potential. Learn about the newest books in spiritual guidance, natural healing, astrology, occult philosophy, and more. Enjoy book reviews, new age articles, a calendar of events, plus current advertised products and services. To get your free copy of *Llewellyn's New Worlds of Mind and Spirit*, send your name and address to:

Llewellyn's New Worlds of Mind and Spirit
P.O. Box 64383-786, St. Paul, MN 55164-0383, U.S.A.

The Victorian Flower Oracle

The Language of Nature

Patricia Telesco

1994
Llewellyn Publications
St. Paul, Minnesota 55164-0383, U.S.A.

FIRST EDITION
First Printing, 1994

Cover painting by Lori Chilefone
Cover design by Alexandra Lumen
Illustrations in Chapters One and Two by Alexandra Lumen
Book design and layout by Trish Finley

Library of Congress Cataloging-in-Publication Data
Telesco, Patricia, 1960-
    The Victorian flower oracle : the language of nature /
Patricia Telesco.
        p.   cm.
    Includes bibliographical references and index.
    ISBN 0-87542-786-3
    1. Fortunetelling by plants. 2. Fortunetelling by flowers.
3. Plants—Folklore—Miscellanea. 4. Symbolism of flowers—
Miscellanea. I. Title.
BF1891.P56T45   1994
133.3—dc20   93-49090
                                                     CIP

Llewellyn Publications
A Division of Llewellyn Worldwide, Ltd.
P.O. Box 64383, St. Paul, MN 55164-0383

Dedication

To the seers and visionaries of all ages who, with peaceful hearts
and loving souls, bravely gaze into the future in the hope of
granting discernment, today.

Also by Patricia Telesco

A Victorian Grimoire
The Urban Pagan
Llewellyn's 1994 Magical Almanac

Forthcoming

Folkways
A Kitchen Witch's Cookbook
A Witch's Brew

Acknowledgements

Each flower in this book is dedicated to friends, and people who without even knowing it have somehow touched my life. The webs we weave throughout time are sometimes so busy that we don't really get to say thank you to each other or the universe. My words are the only gift I have to return the many kindnesses even "strangers" have given me.

I would also like to thank Carl for giving me the focus I needed to help these pages flow into a unified, functional system, and of course Shadow-Cat for helping me, and many other writers, maintain a quality of work which she simply will not allow to be anything but the best!

To my family: I know it seems sometimes I get too caught up in my work, yet you constantly support me even when my nose is in a book. So, this "bud's" for you (sorry, irresistible pun)!

And finally to the readers of books everywhere. Without you, writers would have no one to share their vision with, and the glory of the printed word, which has given us such richness, would fade. Keep reading!

Table of Contents

INTRODUCTION

The future cannot be hidden or obscured from the intelligent soul, but this perfect knowledge cannot be acquired without divine guidance.

Nostradamus

In a world where rationality and religion alone are often inadequate for all our answers, there comes a mixture of feelings regarding fate, superstition, luck, and legend. So, when we consider creating a technique of divining by natural objects, we should also thoughtfully weigh these feelings as they have developed over thousands of years, side by side with humanity. In the examination process, we cannot help but discover historical facts which belie many preconceived notions about what divination is and how it works.

To illustrate, when most people think of a "diviner," frequently they envision the money-centered carnival worker as portrayed in the cinema. Yet in truth, the people next door may have a deck of Tarot cards or other forms of divining tools, some of which are so common that they may not even be aware of them. For example, a woman may get up in the morning and notice the birds are chirping differently and assume it is going to rain. This is a type of divination by omens and signs. Actually, most of the misconceptions regarding divination come from early forms of organized religion that saw not only this but other "psychic" or "magical" phenomena as a threat to their control of the people, instead of a wondrous gift from the Creator.

In making or working with any oracle, the first thing you must remember is that divination is far older than Christianity. With the advent of writing in Sumer around 3000 B.C., we see the first evidence of divination practices, which by this time are already well-developed, leading to the hypothesis that such techniques were probably first designed as soon as man developed an understanding of the idea of a future.

The use of natural objects in divination is also widely known. From gazing on water to the sound of fire cracking, almost everything readily available in the world around our ancestors could, and often did, become a tool both on the mundane and metaphysical level. To understand this, we must first realize that faith in omens, signs, and superstition was common throughout history, and indeed was taken very seriously as almost a science unto itself. Add to this the fact that a majority of people were farmers, depending on the land and its bounty for another day's life, and you can quickly see where a common plant could rise in stature, especially on symbolic levels.

From the time when humanity began simply trying to understand the cycle of life and death right up to present day, traditional "wives' tales" and other assorted advice regarding plants, especially flowers or herbs, was shared from generation to generation. To a people whose life spans were shortened considerably by malnutrition, poor hygiene, and disease, the reliance on superstition was regarded as one way to reclaim a little control over the whims of fate. This dependence was, of course, periodically aided by economic opportunists.

For example, when the ingenious Arab spice traders met the Europeans during the Crusades, they quickly recognized a potentially lucrative situation: an environment full of magic, omens, and witchcraft, which was ripe for harvesting. They used their wisdom and cunning to spread fantastic stories about their spices (laden with a heavy portion of actual Arabic folk tales) to raise the value of their trade. No matter the Arab intention however, the common people employed the renowned magical significance of herbs, spices, flowers, and all manner of natural objects for boon and bane as needed.

In medieval Europe, parsley was eaten to prevent drunkenness, anise for nightmares, basil for animosity, and laurel was taken to invoke the gift of prophesy. It was also believed that heliotrope placed under the head of someone who had been robbed would reveal the thief in a dream that night, and that vervain could aid in foretelling the fate of sick people when placed on their heads by a true healer. Many of these "magical" herbs could be found in the medieval kitchen for culinary use as well.

Another interesting illustration of these types of convictions regarding plants and herbs comes to us from China. Because of the longevity of the yarrow plant and the number of stalks which are produced from one root, the yarrow became rather infamous and was regarded with awe. Around the advent of the Christian era, a system of divination which employed yarrow stalks was discovered in written records.

In most texts, the basic procedure was to take fifty stalks and throw one randomly away. Then this pile was split into two without regard to the number of stalks apiece. After this, the piles were reduced systematically by four stalks each until the number of stalks that remained was zero to four. From these, the diviner formed a line. This whole process was repeated six times until a hexagram was formed.

The throw that resulted in a particular hex could not be regarded as chance to minds which accepted direct intervention between the seen and unseen worlds. And while they sometimes found difficulty in relating all facets and changes of the natural world to a mere sixty-four hexes, by 136 B.C. an Imperial authority arranged for a special study on the "Changes of Chou," which was the fundamental study for this divinatory practice. In 2 A.D. the various writings of the Changes of Chou became collectively known as the I Ching, and was also approached as a philosophical system. This divinatory system is still in popular use today.

I mention this here so that you begin to see how diverse the history of divination, specifically that which employs plants, really is. There have literally been hundreds of methods devised over the centuries. Cromniomancy is divination by observation of growth in specially prepared onions. Daphnomancy portends fortune by the sound of burning laurel leaves. Botanomancy employs burning briar or vervain branches, phyllorhodomancy, the sounds of rose leaves clapped against the hand, sycomancy, dried fig leaves, and xylomancy looks to the appearance of fallen tree branches, the position of burning logs, randomly thrown sticks and/or straw to answer the querent's questions.

No matter what the method, however, we see that humanity has consistently turned to the natural world to try and find answers to the questions nagging at their hearts. The instructions and interpretations in this book are presented to you first to reconnect you with that Gaia-spirit by familiarizing you with the folklore surrounding flowers, trees, and herbs, and ideas on how to use this information for modern magic. Secondly, it is shared to impart many of the wonderful recipes devised for various forms of greenery throughout the ages. Lastly, it is offered as a practical way to make a divining tool permeated with this richness for those moments when we find we need an aid to give us perspective.

The advantages of creating your own oracle are many. The first is the fact that you can formulate a magical implement which is filled with your own vision and talent, making the finished tool even more useful and effective in your hands. Secondly, the time you spend on developing the system will increase the latent personal energy in the oracle, again making it responsive specifically to you. I also think you will generally find the process very informational and satisfying. This is no less so with the suggested recipes and applications.

Any time you give physical form to a concept it helps you improve your concentration and gives deeper understanding of your own perceptions, especially as they pertain to the subject involved. Through these pages you will have the opportunity to consider exactly what you want from your finished oracle (or culinary treat), then fashion one appropriately suited to your Path and needs.

As with any divination system, this alone cannot be a guru for your entire existence, only your heart can fill that job. However, by allowing yourself to experiment with the recipes and employ the finished device as a focus, the cards, stones, or edibles may give you a fresh outlook and understanding that alluded you before.

This is the greatest gift of divining tools. It is a gift which comes from the abundance of Mother herself: the ability to step back for a moment and regard our questions, situations, and lives with new insight. We can then reapproach our circumstances with a refreshed heart to effect creative, positive solutions.

CHAPTER ONE

Creating the Oracle

Let me see it in a dream, or let it be discovered by divination, or let a divinely inspired man declare it.

Hittite prayer of Mursil II

The first, most obvious question to come to many readers' minds is, "Why a Victorian oracle?" The inspiration for this effort was twofold. First was my unsuccessful personal quest to find a divination system which really sang the song of my heart. While there are many good ones on the market, Robin Wood's Tarot being closest to my own personal vision, none of them seemed to have that elusive edge which could coax my higher senses into signalling a resounding "yes."

Second was the fact that during the writing of *A Victorian Grimoire* I became spellbound by the language of plants, specifically flowers. The creative uses for various petals, and the joy exhibited in such activities by the people of this era, was nothing less than inspirational to someone already fond of herbal arts. Put these two incidents together and voilà! A book and totally unique form of divination was born.

For those who have not read *A Victorian Grimoire*, it is helpful to understand the importance of flowers, trees, and herbs to this period in history (approximately 1850-1910). They not only appear reminiscent of the

1

lacy, romantic atmosphere prevalent during these days, but were an integral part of culinary arts, home medical treatment, perfumery, and literally hundreds of other domestic applications important for the ever-frugal housewife. So much was the case, that most homes were not complete without a floral garden useful for far more than just accenting the landscape.

Besides the more mundane applications, flowers, herbs, trees, and all manner of natural objects also appeared frequently in Victorian art, decorating, and gentle hobbies of the home front. The Victorian lady of means might have wiled away the free hours of her day by making small flower books, interlaced with tender poetry and sayings as a special gift for a friend, or to pass on to her daughter. Frequently these buds were from her own gardening efforts, so that the final product was doubly meaningful. It seemed that no matter where you looked, bits of earthy environment filled almost every portion of the Victorian life and home with a sentimental ambience.

This almost zealous veneration towards the spirit of beauty so captured my interest that I began to do more research into the origins of the Victorian floral language and folklore of the plant world in general. The first thing I discovered is that the language of flowers *is not* limited to just blossoms. In many instances trees and other plants such as moss or vines, that we don't usually associate as "flowers," are included in this vernacular. This was wonderful because it increased the number of prospective symbols available for an oracle and, consequently, the variety of personalized interpretations which could be achieved.

Secondly, I found that the tradition of ascribing symbolism to items in the natural world is a very old practice, based on the idea that the divine being could best communicate lessons through the beautiful creation of nature. This conviction is one which evidences itself strongly in any positive spiritual lifestyle, and therefore makes an excellent medium for a visionary tool. As it happens, there was even a method of divining by the lines in a pansy petal devised during the Victorian era. It is no small wonder then that this period in history is also sometimes fittingly called "the age of flowers."

Finally, it seems that blossoms and plants lend themselves easily to various types of handcrafts which can be employed towards formulating your own divinatory device. If you find that the approaches presented herein are not ones which you perceive as working well for you, I have described in Chapter Seven some alternative oracles and additional symbols which you can easily apply.

For the purpose of this text, I will be sharing ideas for making something similar to a Tarot deck or rune set, but with fewer characters, which may be easier to handle and memorize than the seventy-two characters of a customary Tarot. The size of the final oracle really will be up to you, but it should include at least twenty-five distinctive cards or stones (the traditional number of symbols in a set of Viking runes) to allow for enough versatility.

The expanse of human experience is not going to be represented easily within twenty-five archetypal images. This is why your intuitive skills are very important not only to the actual readings produced by the oracle, but also to the way it is created. Basically, you will be trying to develop a system which gives enough surface information to spark generalized insight, then leaves the remaining perceptions to the hands and eyes of a capable diviner—namely you!

The Decoupage Oracle

The first thing you will need to create this deck is either some sturdy art paper, cardboard, or a blank set of cards (which are often available at hobby shops), and some good quality art spray to help increase the longevity of your creation. In the interest of being ecologically mindful, use recycled paper products for your base if possible. This way your oracle will reflect a healthy respect for nature in both depiction and substructure.

If at any point during the process you are uncertain as to what products are best to use, ask for assistance at the nearest art or office supply store. The clerks should be well-trained enough to give you guidance. An alternative is to ask for suggestions from a nearby school art instructor.

The next thing to decide is how fancy you want to get. The decoupage deck can be easily created with photographs or clip art prepared in collage-style with little fuss. If you decide on this approach, your major difficulty will be finding all the pictures you want. As starting points, I suggest home and garden publications, seed catalogs, field guides to herbs or flowers, or even photographs taken of local greenhouses or a neighbor's bountiful floral landscaping. A photocopier can be the handiest tool for your decoupage deck so that you don't have to cut up treasured books, and indeed you may even want to use some of the art within these pages. In this instance, you can color the clip art before assembly to suit your personal taste.

In Chapters Four, Five, and Six of this book you will find listed many of the plants from the Victorian language of flowers from which to choose, and watch for, while you are searching. Remember, your deck can have all of these or only those that you personally choose, but try and create a minimum of twenty-five cards to improve the randomness of your oracle as well as the diversity of explication.

If your background is not precut, trim your base cards into a comfortable size for your hand. For many people three inches by five inches works very well, and as a matter of fact, blank three-by-five cards can also be your base! Once these blanks are assembled, it is best to work on only one symbol at a time. This way all your personal energy and attention is on the meaning of that distinctive plant and how it should correlate to the construction of the card.

Next, consider if you want the background of the card to remain blank or to be colored. Magic markers, paints, and even scraps of fabric can be used to cover the backing if you wish. However, make sure you don't overload your cards with so many layers that they become too thick, bulky, and difficult to shuffle. If you use fabric, put it only on the visual side of the card, glued securely in place. To save yourself a step, purchase tinted art board instead of white, in your chosen background color.

Take your photographs or clip art and lay them on the card. Try a couple different placements and arrangements until it feels right. As you assemble it, ponder the meanings of each flower or plant you've chosen. Try and keep these associations strongly in mind while you work so that the card itself takes on those specific energies.

If you happen to be talented enough to paint or draw each card yourself, all the better! This will increase your focus and help direct your magical goals. However, this should not discourage the individual who is not as artistically inclined from making a deck. The feeling you put into and receive from your creation will be the most important factor to its effectiveness, not how other people perceive it.

If for some reason you feel a card should have a different meaning than what's described, definitely follow your own inner voice. Next to the production mechanism itself, this is one of the best ways you can personalize your oracle. The only caution is to be certain to note this specialized connotation and keep it accessible for future reference. A small, three-ring binder functions well for the task since you easily can carry it with you. This binder can double later as a readings journal where your layouts and successes can be transcribed.

Once you have defined the symbolism of the plant for your readings, this interpretation needs to be your primary center of attention in the way you orchestrate the card. For example, the dandelion has no reversed position as discussed in this book. If you decide to use this interpretation, you may wish to find an overhead shot of the dandelion and place it in the exact center of the card so that the visual effect is analogous to the functional meaning. Then, glue your images to the backing. On the other hand, if you decide to write an alternative interpretation of the dandelion which includes a reversed position, you might glue the picture of the flower standing in grass on the backing so that there is a definitive inverted position. (See the illustration on the following page.)

After your flowers are secured in the chosen positions, print or calligraph the name onto the card so it is immediately recognizable. My handwriting is a little difficult to read, so I typed nice labels and adhered them to the cards as well. Press-apply lettering is a very nice option too, and can be obtained frequently in the craft section of your local five-and-dime. For the more enterprising individual, you can add two to three drops of essential oil to your inks and have an oracle which is as full of aroma as the various plants it represents!

Once the glue is dry, I suggest spraying the card with a protective art spray before applying any clear varnish or lacquer. This will help preserve the colors and shades in the chosen pictures from the sometimes harsh chemicals of the coating. The choice of glossy or flat lacquer is yours, but I find the flat finish shows off the pictures better. Finally, allow the card to dry on a clean, lint-free surface. It doesn't hurt to put it underneath a cake glass to keep hair and dust away from the varnish until it is dry.

Repeat the process with each card, remembering that the most important part of your project is not necessarily that of creating a visually

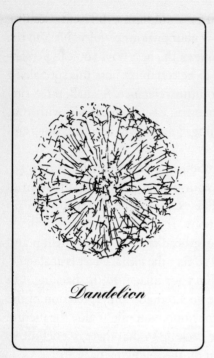

Overhead view

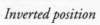

Inverted position

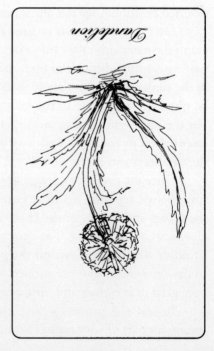

impressive piece of art. Sometimes the simplest tools are the most enjoyable and regularly used. If you don't think so, just ask any child why he or she plays with pots or old boxes instead of an expensive or flashy toy. When the work is completed, if you have a deck that is deeply meaningful to you, then you have accomplished your task exceedingly well.

The Pressed Flower Oracle

Another way of making your deck, which is more complex but just as rewarding, is using waxed or pressed-dried flowers and leaves instead of clip art. The latter was a very popular Victorian method for decorating keepsake books. If you carefully search the pages of a book from the early 1900s you will frequently discover a rose, violet, clover, or other dried snippet waiting to surprise you. These waxed or dried leaves and buds, as long as they are *flat*, will function very well in your oracle.

You may want to grow and dry your own flowers so that your deck is even more personally meaningful. Once harvested, there are several good techniques you can use to press flowers, not the least of which is to purchase a gadget available through Co-Op America (2100 M Street N.W., Suite 403, Box 18217, Washington DC 20036). This wonderful device allows you to dry and press a wide variety of items within about three weeks. The price ($12.95) includes a booklet of instructions and ideas.

On the other hand, if you are the proverbial do-it-yourself type (ah, a Victorian in disguise), there are means to create functional presses at home. The historical methods instruct to lay your ferns, buds, leaves, or mosses between sheets of blotting paper as soon after picking as possible. Be sure that any moisture on the leaves is dried off so that they do not discolor or mold. Arrange your plants on the paper with care, making sure not to overlap and separating according to their texture and color. Ferns cannot be pressed too firmly, as any flower with more pithy textures.

Your pressing device may also be of Victorian fashioning. In this instance you would place each layer of plants atop one another on a piece of board with at least four to six pieces of paper between each layer. Then position another piece of wood on top, strapping the whole bundle together to look like a bound book (old belts work exceptionally well for this).

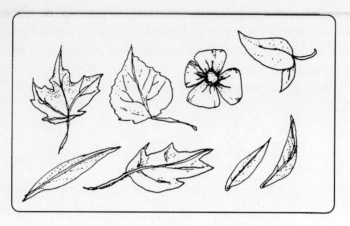

Leaves and flowers laid out on blotting paper.
*(Be sure they **do not** touch each other.)*

Belt or strap

Wood

Paper

Plants

The press

You should change the blotting paper at least twice in a two-week period for best results. If any of your plants adhere to the paper, a simple tap on the back of the page should loosen them. Mosses and seaweed are about the only exceptions to this rule, the former needing only to be placed in thick paper for pressing once, and the latter dried quickly by the fire so it will not lose its color.

As a side note, if you don't want to get quite this intricate in your flower pressing efforts, you can try using an old book in much the same manner as the press. In this instance, you would place your petals between two pages, with several pages in between each layout of blooms and leaves, then close the cover of the book. It may be necessary to place straps around the book or another heavy publication on top of the first to add extra weight. You may remove the straps or weight in about fourteen days, but the plants should be left to sit for another forty-eight hours before exposing them to air.

Waxing your component plants is a simpler process yet. Begin by picking the item and letting it dry a little in the sun. You don't want your blossom to turn brown, but you do need it fairly free of moisture for waxing to be successful. Waxing is best done with plant parts that are already semi-flat such as leaves, fronds, and singular flower petals (wax enough of the petals so you can arrange them to look like a whole flower).

Once the plant is dried off, put it between two pieces of waxed paper (waxed side towards the plant) and turn your iron on a low, warm setting. You do not want the heat applied to be drastic or it will burn your greenery. Gingerly touch the iron to the wax paper over the plant to check the temperature. If it melts the wax and leaves the plant with near to its original color, you have the right temperature. Unfortunately, you may have to try a couple of times to get the process just right. Open the sheets of waxed paper and loosen the herbage while the wax is still warm or your plant will be stuck inside! If this should happen, don't despair, simply warm the sheets again until they release your treasure.

After pressing or waxing your chosen plants, you can then return to the backing for the cards, arranging, gluing, and varnishing for a lovely decoupage effect. An alternative to varnish, with which I have had some success, is to instead adhere a thin layer of clear plastic over the plants cut in the same size as the card backing. The only real problem with this method is that the plastic tends to scratch after a while, and the edges can be rough on the hands. I also feel that plastic does not present as pleasant a finished look as the varnish.

The Wood or Stone Oracle

The Victorian language of flowers is very versatile. Besides the decks mentioned above, you can also try preparing wood slices or stones of a similar size and shape. This set will be closer in appearance to a collection of runes. The major advantages to employing either of these as your base are found in the durability of the materials and ease of transporting same. Stone and wood will withstand much more abuse than paper, even paper of a good quality, and can be carried in a pouch wherever you go.

The main thing to be aware of in choosing your medium is that your wood slices or stones need to be large enough to house a dry flower or picture, just as with the cards. They also need to be almost identically formed so that you cannot recognize them by feel when doing a reading. This would hinder the randomness in the divinatory process.

As you gather your wood or stones, give thanks to the land for its gift to you. Timber is best taken from large fallen branches, being already dried and released from the trees. For rock, beach stones make an excellent choice since they are smooth and frequently flat.

Once collected, you can follow exactly the same procedures as you did for the cards, except the wood should be properly sanded so it is soft to the touch, stones need to be washed completely before applying any varnish, and your glue should be appropriate to your base material. Wood and stone both may be painted for background coloration, however you may wish to choose your base medium in diverse natural shades to begin with to eliminate this step. While you will not have as large a space in which to arrange your pictures or dried flowers, the finished appearance is really quite lovely, adding the extra pleasure of having your divination tool be a tribute to the bounty of the land!

Top view   *Side view*

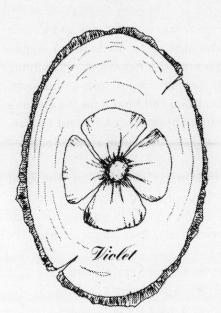 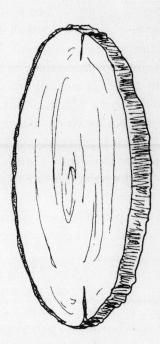

Wood slices—taken from a fairly large branch.
*(Varnish **both** sides of the wood and the edges for easier handling.)*

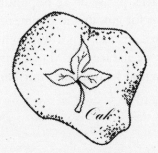 

Stones—singular leaves or buds are best for small stones.

Preparing the Finished Oracle for Use

When you have completed all the symbols you want for your oracle, take the time to set them on your altar and bless them. To do this, I suggest preparing your sacred space however is most comfortable to you, lighting white candles (a color of protection and pure intentions), and perhaps burning incense which consists of dandelion and broom for the divining arts, angelica for vision, and cinnamon to bring success to your endeavors. Obviously your choice of herbs can vary, and can be chosen from the suggestions in Chapter Three.

At this point is it nice to say a little prayer while holding your hand over the finished oracle. As you share your intended purpose for this tool with your patron god and goddess, visualize white light pouring into each symbol so that only good may come of their use. One such prayer might be:

> *Lady and Lord, I bring before you the work of my hands. I ask that you bless it as a tool which will grant insight and wisdom when my vision is clouded, or when a friend needs aid. When in use, I pray that the intuitive energies will flow freely, unhindered by personal opinions and that the information shared will always be for the greatest good. So mote it be.*

As with all magical rites, change the wording so it is comfortable on your lips and reflects the true sentiments of your heart. When you are done blessing the deck, place it safely away as you would any cherished magical tool, with proper respect and thoughtfulness.

When the time comes to use the oracle, please do so responsibly. The beauty of such a creation is not meant for gloom and doom, or to help change things to your way of thinking. Instead it is a way to help yourself or a friend through the confusions we all face from time to time. Most importantly, remember this is a magical instrument your hands have created. Enjoy it!

CHAPTER TWO

How to Use the Oracle

The guess of the wise is truth.

Icelandic proverb

This oracle can be used in conjunction with almost any of the traditional Tarot or rune spreads, as long as they don't exceed the total number of symbols you have created for your basic structure. However, this divination system has been created rather uniquely. Therefore, it is good to have available to you some alternative layouts, reflective of this distinctive process. To these ends, and to offer you greater flexibility, you may want to try the original layouts created and described herein, specifically for the language of flowers.

If you are not already familiar with the Tarot or runes, it would be worth your time to read a book or two on these subjects, if for no other reason than just to acquaint yourself with the variety of readings which can be done and associated symbolism. Llewellyn Publications offers several books, including *Tarot Spells* and *A Guide to the Runes*, which can be of tremendous assistance. I mention this because, while you have not developed a "traditional" Tarot deck, the function and form is similar enough to be workable in that construct, as well as with numerous standard rune casts.

Before you begin, though, I do recommend looking through the entire oracle again, one symbol at a time. Meditate on the emblem for a few moments and see if you get any feelings or impressions from it. If so, note them then read the descriptions which follow. I recommend this because I truly believe that in order for a divination system to be useful it must make sense to you.

If your interpretation of a card/stone is different than those given in this book, by all means use it! Your intuitive sense of how your oracle should be deciphered in any reading is very important to the overall success of your divining efforts. I will remind you again, however, to write down your clarification of the card/stone and keep it handy. You must keep the meanings consistent, except when changed by neighboring symbols, if you want your system to function well.

Another reason for taking the time to closely survey the completed product is simply to help endow your new oracle with augmented personal energy. The more you handle the components, look at them, think about them ... the more this tool becomes *yours*. It is like having a special chair in your home where you always sit after work and everyone *knows* that seat is "Mom's." Your divining tools, with time, can become that specialized and attuned to your touch, especially considering this particular one has been made by your own hands.

Besides meditating on the symbols, I also suggest having a special place to keep them when not in use. For one thing, this keeps unwanted hands from haphazardly examining them. It also helps preserve your magical tool from any unusual energies so that each time you use it it is "clean" of residual emotions, etc. A natural fiber pouch, wooden box, scrap of silk, or even a satin scarf all make excellent wraps because they are closely linked to the organic world. This particular divinatory device definitely offers one means to "get back to nature," even from your city apartment!

Like any system of divination, certain traditional methods of handling Tarot decks and runes have come to us through the ages. Generally speaking for decks, you begin with the entire set of cards in your hands while a silent question is posed either by you or the querent. I say silent because then the querent can be certain that your reading is not being influenced by what you may already know about his or her situation. However, if it helps to clarify the reading, the question can be spoken out loud after you have given your initial perceptions. This is really a matter of personal preference.

The deck is then shuffled thoroughly and cut three times by the left hand (closest to the heart). The querent at this point picks one of the piles at random, still concentrating on the question. This pile goes on *top* of the other two. You are now basically ready to begin. The only item remaining is that of a significator.

The significator is the card which represents the querent. This card can be chosen in one of two ways. The first is at random, pulling it from the deck and placing it at the center of the reading. Second is to review the meanings of the cards to try and find one which, in its upright position, best represents the individual. Look for the strongest personality traits, compared to the interpretation of various cards in the deck, to make your decision. If you use the second method, you can continue to employ this card for that particular person each time you read for him or her.

Before you actually begin the reading I usually advise that you remind yourself and the querent that divination is not the end-all and be-all of spiritual understanding. Its purpose is not to act as your conscious or personal teacher. It is only meant to help give you better perspective, and hopefully insight. What you do with the information gained is totally up to you, for right or wrong. Don't blame the "cards" if life hands you a lemon. As the old saying goes, make lemonade, then consult the cards to see what they say about the underlying energy currents bringing sour fruit your way!

When you do your actual layout you will notice that the interpretation of the floral language is written in the present tense. So, if the almond card, for example, lands in the position of the past in the reading, the explication of it will be altered slightly to reflect that position. In this instance it might indicate that the querent has recently made a hasty decision which is influencing his or her reading and present circumstances. Reversed in the past position, the almond portends a period of depression coming to an end. In this way, you may use your deck for a wide range of expression and interpretation, allowing your vision and intuition to play a definitive role for the readings done.

As for the runes, almost everyone has a slightly different way of handling them. I like to keep mine wrapped in silk, then use this cloth to lay them on as they are chosen for the reading. Whatever approach you feel most comfortable with is the one you should choose, but I do suggest having some physical contact with the stones while the question is being pondered.

Significators can be chosen in the same manner as in Tarot, and the rest of the routine, with the exception of "cutting" the deck, is really pretty much the same for both structures. The only difficulty you may encounter with runes is the fact that your stone may not be pulled exactly in an upright or reversed position. If this happens, I suggest turning the rune to whichever position it is closest to clockwise (the direction of unhindered, flowing time). (Refer to the illustration on page 17.)

Neither system (runes or Tarot) is better than the other; only different. You will know in time which feels more comfortable to your hands. I generally prefer runes, but know many people who would rather go to the dentist than give up their Tarot cards.

As you work with your oracle, you may also observe yourself following certain routines before a reading; a ritual of sorts. Perhaps you light a candle, play music, burn some incense, or mark your change in demeanor with any number of other concentration aids. When you see these develop, keep them! Repetition of sound, light, scent, or any other "sensual" input helps train the mind to lose itself from the mundane and focus on the world just outside our normal range of understanding.

Another recommendation I would like to make is that you consider maintaining a small journal of your personal readings. While it is usually not wise to do layouts for yourself if you are upset (the negative energy is carried over into the way you discern the cards chosen), doing periodic general readings for yourself can be very rewarding. By retaining this information in a journal, you can return to it any time and see how accurate and successful your intuitive work is becoming. Just like any tool, it takes time and practice to become adept, but through a well-kept divination diary you can actually monitor your progress.

Besides acting as a measure of your own prophetic talents, the journal also becomes a place to watch your spiritual growth. As time goes on, you will generally find that the early deliberations in your diary seem almost simple compared to the present. Your personal reflections about each reading will grow and change to reveal subtle transformations in

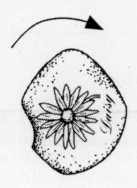

Pulled sideways → turned clockwise is upright.

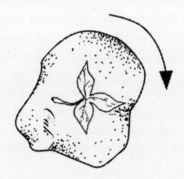
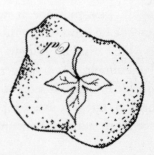

Pulled sideways → turned clockwise is inverted.

your soul's journey, which might otherwise have gone unnoticed. In this way, your work with the oracle not only grants insight for various pressing situations, but also encourages you along your Path by helping improve your awareness of self-development.

Sample Layouts

In the interest of simplicity, I have written these layouts as if I were talking about a Tarot deck. If you have chosen to make the runic form of the oracle instead, simply place the runes you pull for the reading in the same patterns as shown for the cards, and interpret them accordingly. Or, if you have a handful of plants recently gathered from outdoors, close your eyes and choose one at a time, laying them out in the same manner.

The Daily Guidance Layout

This reading is done in the same manner as some people might check their horoscope in the morning, inspect the clouds to predict the weather, or pull a rune and read the interpretation to gain insight on what the day holds for them. In this case, try to clear your mind of any questions other than those which pertain to your activities that day. Shuffle the cards thoroughly, then pull one at random and read the explanation in this book (or the one you have written yourself); respond to various circumstances which arise accordingly.

For example, if you happen to be going on a job interview and pull honeysuckle inverted, it seems to indicate that you may encounter a lack of honesty or integrity at some point during the day. Because of this, you might be more cautious about any offers that appear "too good to be true."

The Past, Present, and Future Layout
(Foundation, Action, and Outcome)

This is the most simple reading to do, other than the previous one. It is best applied in conjunction with uncomplicated matters where you are concerned about the outcome. The significator is placed at (A). The first card from the top of the deck is placed at (B) which is the position of the past, or what is at the base of the situation. The second card goes at the apex (C) for the present and actions called for. The final card (D) is the outcome or the immediate future.

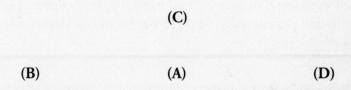

(C)

(B)   **(A)**   **(D)**

From this position the significator can affect all cards. The card in position (C) will be the most predominant influence on the querent. However, the card at (B) can affect how much this influence is felt. Likewise, (C) influences (D) so that you get a flow of reading instead of stagnant images.

Sample Reading

Question: How will my move to New York affect my relationships?
Reading: (A) jasmine reversed (drawn randomly)
           (B) zinnia upright
           (C) buttercup upright
           (D) carnation upright

Interpretation

Self: A need presently to rely on your own sensibilities. Don't trust anything which seems too good to be true. A caution to scrutinize your decisions. Someone nearby may not be totally honest with you.

Past Base: The zinnia upright is usually a card of friendship but since it is in the past position here, I would say that either a friend has recently moved away, or a friendship is soon to end for one reason or another. Since the card is upright, the ending is not bitter or angry, but one of necessity.

In this position the zinnia also indicates the heart of your question, that of relationships.

Present Action: An improvement in financial situations, this may indicate that your move was for a new job, or will produce employment which is better than you have had up until now. On the other hand this card counsels patience in all things. It may take you a little while to build new friendships in a strange place, but the upright position of the card portends they will come, when you least expect it.

Future: Success! Social occasions, admiration of business acquaintances—this card would tend to indicate your move is a very beneficial one both personally and professionally. Move forward with confidence, relying on your instincts to guide you.

The Four Winds Layout

Again connecting with the natural world, this reading's interpretations correspond to the significance placed on the four winds (also major compass points). You begin with your significator in the center (A), then follow it to the east (B) where the sun rises, south (E), west (D) and finally north (C).

(E)

(D)   **(A)**   **(B)**

(C)

The major inter-relationships here are between points (D) and (B) and (C) and (E), with minor influences felt (C) to (B), (B) to (E), (E) to (D), and (D) to (C) (clockwise).

Beginning in the east, with the rising sun we find the wind of intellect, business, and revitalization. This is the card of more mundane matters, concerns of the mind, education, etc., and portends the general climate with regard to these as they relate to your question.

The southern wind is one of power, drastic change, and strength. This card will indicate what is your greatest ally, source of creative energy, or what changes you may have to face to bring about positive resolutions. Because of its ferocity, the southern card is the indicator of the whole person (body, mind, and spirit).

The western wind is cool and moist, one which indicates the most fertile projects for the querent right now. Since this breeze greets us like a soothing balm, it may also give counsel on a situation which needs healing. This is also a spiritual wind, and may give the querent reflections on his or her Path.

Finally, the northern wind brings the chill of winter. It indicates outmoded ideas or habits which should be worked on, and is also the wind which may indicate needs associated with physical health.

Sample Reading

Question: Why do I seem to be repeating cycles in my relationships?
Reading: (A) evergreen upright (drawn randomly)
          (B) iris reversed
          (C) clover upright
          (D) balm upright
          (E) holly reversed

Interpretation

Self: The upright evergreen in this scenario speaks strongly of the querent's relationship to him or herself. It would tend to indicate that the problem with relationships has to do with a lack of self-confidence and esteem. The questioner may be so unsure of him or herself that he or she makes others ill at ease, and thus relationships are rocky at best.

East: The iris reversed speaks of taking on too many projects and spreading yourself too thin. With relationship to the self card, I would say that the querent's lack of self worth is causing him or her to try to impress people by being a terminal volunteer. The counsel here is to slow down and do one thing really well, instead of several things poorly.

South: To your advantage, you have an amazing amount of personal energy and creative ideas to bring to any endeavor. This is your strong suit; being able to see marvelous possibilities and/or opportunities. However, with regard to your eastern card, this may also add to your desire to accomplish more than you possibly can with the hours in a day. Since you have vision, the need here is to narrow it down and find focus. Once you do, eventual success cannot help but follow.

West: Your personal need for support and positive input. Here the healing needed is again internal, as spoken of with the self card. The time for reconciling childhood doubts has come. You are being guided to place the past in perspective so you can move forward with new confidence. Because of its position in the spread, I would also say the balm indicates a strong tendency towards the gift of healing in your spiritual life. Pay attention to those urges to help others, as long as you also remember to help yourself.

North: Get out of the habit of speaking before you think. This card would seem to indicate that part of your difficulty with relationships has a great deal to do with ineffectual or misunderstood communications. More than likely, this tendency comes from being insecure with your own ideas having merit. Relax, realize that you have good concepts, and present them calmly. Once you believe in yourself, those around you will listen more closely to your words, discovering great treasures there!

The Five Petal Layout (the Pentagram)

This layout is meant to attune itself to more spiritual matters. The five points of the petals, done in the same fashion as a pentagram, represent the elements of Air, Earth, Fire, Water, and Spirit (also sometimes called Ether or Void).

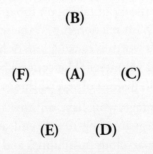

In the position of Air (B) are the psychic influences in your life right now. This card also deals with the conscious mind, and matters of careful consideration. The apex of the question or situation.

Earth (C) speaks of our physical being, growth, monetary matters, and the creative spark within.

Fire (D) is a purifier, energy, and usually the heating up of some specific situation to bring growth and change.

Water (E) shares of hidden matters, things just beneath the surface of the situation, the unconscious mind, and especially emotions.

Spirit (F) is the transformation, the outcome of the situation or question once the progression from B to E has been completed.

Sample Reading

Question: Should I join this study group?
Reading: (A) almond upright (drawn randomly)
          (B) daisy upright
          (C) buttercup reversed
          (D) fennel upright
          (E) myrtle upright
          (F) carnation upright

Interpretation

Self: A hopefulness regarding the situation, but hope which may not be balanced with perspective. An opportunity exists, but it may not be the one in front of your nose. The counsel here is take your time in making any decisions.

Air: A sense of innocence surrounds you along with pure intentions. This would indicate that you want to go into the group for the right reasons, now the only question is if it is the correct gathering for you.

Earth: A warning against trusting your first impressions of anything, especially those that are financial in nature. If this group is asking for money to join, the advice would be to first examine how the funds are used to be certain everything is "on the level."

Fire: Old habits and fears which have bothered you are now ready to be rooted out. Perhaps you are afraid of speaking up in groups, or nervous around people in general. This card indicates that somehow whatever decision you make about this group will also allow you new freedom in other areas of your life.

Water: Something that you have desired or worked for is about to come true. While you may have felt swayed by your lack of progress up until now, don't give up. You simply aren't *seeing* the growth, even though it is there, just below the water's edge. Perseverance and patience are called for to bring it to full view.

Spirit: Admiration, social occasions, joy! This card portends a very favorable outcome for your decision. People will look at you in a new light, and you may even find your sense of self improves greatly.

The Six Petal Layout (the Hexagram)

The significator is placed at (A). Position (B) represents the overview of the situation and significant influences on same. (C) is matters of the recent past affecting the question at hand. At (D) we have the present. This position often reveals the emotions, actions, or thoughts of the querent with regard to their question. (E) is the card of hidden current, the unseen. Here things which may have been overlooked are revealed as a basis to the question. (F) represents the actions called for in the present or near future, and (G) is your outcome card.

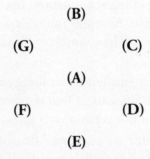

(B)

(G)   **(C)**

(A)

(F)   **(D)**

(E)

Sample Reading
Question: Should I accept the new position just offered?
Reading: (A) dandelion (drawn randomly)
          (B) honeysuckle upright
          (C) lilac reversed
          (D) fennel upright
          (E) clover reversed
          (F) moss reversed
          (G) myrtle upright

Interpretation

Self: A feeling of uncertainty and nervousness. For some reason you are ill at ease about the company or work you have been offered. This card is neither positive nor negative, but simply one that speaks of fate's hand at work.

Overview: A counsel to trust in yourself to do the right thing. This is the card of honest dealings and integrity. No matter what everyone else says, you need to listen to your inner voice and follow through.

Past: A passion or interest which consumed much of your time and attention, possibly at the expense of equally important matters. Your actions during this period are having a direct effect on what is occurring presently.

Present: An herb of protection and strength, I would say that this card indicates a personal concern as to whether or not you are properly equipped to handle the position offered.

Foundation: Frustration, bad luck, and awkward circumstances. Whatever has lead up to this job offer, it has been like a whirlwind which you haven't quite caught up to yet. Everything is happening too fast for you to get a good perspective. I also feel that this relates directly to position (C), where personal actions may have lead to the feelings of frustration.

Action: A caution against being naive or capricious regarding a specific situation. Don't get so caught up in the moment that you lose your perspective. Take a critical look at your actions and motivations, then make your decisions.

Outcome: Whatever your decision, stand by it zealously. Here your devotion and convictions will bring you respect, even from people who might initially disagree with your decision. Don't give up!

The Full Flower Layout

This is a fairly detailed spread especially good for inquiries that are of a complex nature, and those which require more than a simple "yes" or "no" answer. Here, (S) is the individual which is best chosen randomly for this spread. This position indicates the querent's mood or prevalent thoughts. (A) is the base of the flower, and thus the root of the problem or situation. This is the most difficult card in this pattern to read because, like most plant roots, it portends a hidden or unseen matter.

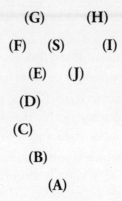

   (B) indicates circumstances or people which promote the difficulty or matter at hand. (C) is the card of obstacles, that which impedes progress or general frustrations. (D) speaks of things in the recent past which may have direct bearing on the situation. (E) is the immediate future if things continue along much the same lines as they have to date.

   (F) is here and now, the present and most personally significant factors in the question at hand. (G) is the card which portrays hopes and fears. (H) portends something or someone where you may find strength and encouragement. (I) is the environment you have to work with and acts as an advice card regarding personal actions, and (J) is the outcome card.

Sample Reading
Question: Am I perusing the best course of action for success with
        my personal talents?
Reading: (A) lavender upright (drawn randomly)
        (B) lilac reversed
        (C) clover reversed
        (D) chamomile upright
        (E) moss upright
        (F) almond upright
        (G) aspen reversed
        (H) daisy upright
        (I) myrtle upright
        (J) holly upright

Interpretation

Base: The answer to your heart's desire is right around the corner. Considering the question at hand, it also portends an offer which you will have to weigh and respond to. Whatever your choice, lavender is a sign that your decision will be an excellent one.

Circumstances: The inverted lilac seems to act as a warning not to completely immerse yourself in your new course of action. Consistency and even-tempered action are what will bring the best results now.

Obstacles: The inverted clover speaks of a brief run of seemingly bad luck. Minor annoyances, unexpected expenditures, and other difficulties may dampen your spirits; but take heart, something good is still to come.

Recent Past: Increased energy for a specific purpose or goal as if you have directed and guided yourself to the attainment of your dreams. Considering the rest of the cards to this point, it seems to be time well spent.

Immediate Future: A new friendship or beneficial acquaintance is soon to appear in your life. Frequently this relationship is on a student-teacher level, so it may pertain directly to a mentor for your talents.

Present: A sign of your anxiousness and hopeful attitude. Don't let your nerves get the best of you. Almond is aligned with the element of Air, and the winds of have definitely begun to move in your life. Be patient.

Hopes/Fears: There is a definite fear in the back of your mind that indicates a lack of self-assurance or even old insecurities nagging at you. The importance of this situation to the rest of your life may seem overwhelming, and bring these anxieties to the forefront of your thoughts. Put them aside and recognize them as simply a by-product of your eagerness and hopes for success, otherwise fear can become an obstacle.

Strength: Your greatest strength may come from your ability to trust as a child, joy in life, and new psychic abilities beginning to evidence themselves. The trust and joy will allow you to meet deterrents with a smile and humor in your back pocket, while your inner voice will provide guidance.

Action: In this position, the myrtle counsels continued zeal and enthusiasm. Even if someone finds fault with your ideas, your devotion to the goal will be greatly respected and aid in the eventual attainment.

Outcome: The holly is an indicator of good wishes and celebration. Again this speaks of your ability to maintain your perspective, organize, and be continually prepared for opportunity. Considering the question and other cards, the course of action you are presently following seems to be bearing fruit. As the old saying goes … if it's not broken, don't fix it! While you may still have to be patient to reap the rewards of your efforts, the victory is indeed sweet!

With regard to these layouts and those commonly associated with Tarot, there is no reason whatsoever that you could not also devise your own patterns to individualize your divination tool even more. In creating these specific readings, I tried to find a visual effect where form and function would match. In other words, the pattern created by the reading looked like the petals of a flower or other items commonly symbolized in magical practices, especially those connected with the natural world.

As with unique interpretations, any layout you personally create should be written down with all its correspondences for your future use. If you find it works extremely well, you may wish to share the pattern with friends who enjoy working with similar divination systems. By so doing, your networking can enrich many lives, including your own.

CHAPTER THREE

The Language of Flowers

*Like plants, most men have hidden properties
that chance alone reveals.*

Duc François de la Rochefoucauld

The Victorian peoples loved their "parlor games" almost as much as their flowers. During this age, all manner of hopeful prophesy routinely appeared alongside noontime teas, dances, and almost any cordial occasion. Something seemed to happen in the general mood of human nature at the turn of the century which caused a growing interest in the occult to the point where mystical experiences were even considered beneficial to mental health. It may have been the honest curiosity to know ones' fate, or the flourishing spirit of individuality, but either way, drawing room divinations became a central part of the Victorian social life and home.

In some ways, this acceptance of the mystical was an unusual dichotomy for a people predominantly Christian in faith. The average person would frequently have been known to follow superstitions, go to tea leaf readers, and observe moon phases for everyday necessities from planting to cutting hair. Very few of these people considered such ideas "magical." Actually, most of them probably gained their knowledge from parents and other family members or friends by way of oral tradition.

Just as in the home, a sprig of some "protective" herb might still be found hanging in the doorway of a village church. In the case of the clerics, such items were looked upon as having divine favor. The common people simply sanctioned what had always been portrayed to them as a truth; the fact that herbs and plants held many marvelous powers to aid a wide variety of needs.

It is because of this extensive acceptance that homeopaths, psychics, and healers could be openly recognized without the fears we know today. Even the mysterious Oriental philosophies were curiously accepted, as brought to the public by Swami Vivekananda through three very well attended lecture tours. This zealous, and somewhat playful, interest in the occult seemed to typify the spiritually hungry atmosphere which existed throughout the era.

By 1889 the need for distraction from difficult, long work days managed to dilute any admonishing voice which might have come from the pulpit, and public exhibitions of mind reading alongside other psychic phenomena became commonplace and very popular. Eva Fay was the most accomplished female spiritualist at the time, often performing in large music halls. A projection telepathist, Wolf Messing, possessed a talent so remarkable that even the scrutinizing eyes of Einstein and Freud could find no fault in his work. People such as these helped encourage the founding of two organizations dedicated to studying psychic phenomena: the Theosophical Society in 1875 and the American Society for Psychical Research in 1885.

On the domestic level, divinatory activities were just as fashionable, the most popular forms were mainly those which could be done without anyone being the wiser. Such examples include divination by moles and graphology (handwriting analysis). Other prevalent approaches included Ouija® boards, palmistry, phrenology (skull conformation analysis), table tipping, and tea leaf readings.

With this perspective, it is understandable that divination techniques as "party games" were so successful. Hundreds of means to discover your future love, determine when to plant or harvest crops, and even predict rainy seasons, were devised by the creative Victorian mind. Perhaps you would meet a strange man who had a mole on his forehead. In the system which prophesied by moles, this meant that the newcomer would someday own many great possessions. This is just one example of literally hundreds of divination approaches found at the turn of the century. There was even a method conceived of divining by dust!

Studying this fascination, in combination with the air of sentimental idealism predominant during these years, makes it easy to see why methods of divination by flowers or herbs would have been developed, especially by these people. Nature was the perfect reflection of God. Therefore, the living organisms of the wild could communicate divine lessons and messages in a beautiful way no human could. This fundamental belief of the divine spark in all things is what gives the Victorian oracle such charm and potency.

Flower and Herb Divinations

We all know the childhood pastime of picking a daisy and saying "s/he loves me, s/he loves me not," or gaily running up to a friend and placing a buttercup under his or her chin to see if he or she likes butter. These types of diversions were no less enjoyed by our ancestors. Flowers and plants of all kinds were scattered happily about the Victorian home in any manner the creative housewife could conceive.

Be they indoors or out, the petals' greatest gift, besides their beauty, may have been the many hours of amusement they shared. One system of flower divination instructs you to go to your garden and gather a small bouquet for yourself. While you pick, consider a specific question much as you would do for a Tarot reading. Return to the house with your flowers in hand, pull out one flower at a time, and look up its meaning. These interpretations could then be written down for a final reading of what the flowers were telling you. The only problem with this method comes with people who, adept in the floral vocabulary, choose plants which would answer their question as they thought best.

Flowers were not the only garden items used for divination, though. Another method known as daphnomancy uses fresh laurel leaves. These are placed in your incense burner (or an open fire) while concentrating on a question. It is said that if the leaves crack loudly and burn brightly that the time is favorable for action. If they smolder and die out, it is not.

Throw a handful in your fireplace all at once and observe the flame. If it grows together in an upward direction, this is also a positive sign. Three flame points mean that circumstances are changing and energies merging, one point is determination or focus, and two flame points mean a friend can help you accomplish your goal. Bay leaves are an appropriate and inexpensive substitute if laurel is not available, as are other herbs which in their magical attributes correspond to the question at hand.

Another way to use plants to divine is by making a pendulum out of them. Take some yarn the length of your hand plus a little extra to tie the leaf, blossom, etc. into it with three knots. Yellow is a common color of yarn for this technique as it is magically associated with the divinatory arts.

Choose your pendulum according to what subject your question reflects. In this instance a bay leaf could be applied to a question regarding the consequences of a situation. Attach the herb securely, then place your elbow on a table with the end of the thread in your dominant hand (the one you write with), continuing to concentrate on the question. If there is no movement after a few minutes, it means that the circumstances are too muddled presently, and no certain answer can be given. Circular movement is considered a positive response; back and forth, negative.

Flower and Herb Applications

The extent to which the flower became revered by people of this era is best evidenced in 1879 when a book by Miss Corruthers of Inverness was dedicated to the language of flowers. This tome became the standard source for flower symbolism both in England and the United States for many years to come. Even today, it is difficult not to find some references to it in modern texts on the subject.

In some respects, various bits of herbage afforded a silent means of communication for lovers of the Victorian years, especially conveying many sentiments that the propriety of the times would not usually allow. Also, anything that carried the scent of a particular plant was considered to extend the same theme. So, should a young lady drop her handkerchief scented with violet, it would be an inconspicuous message that her admiration would be unwavering.

Our Victorian ancestors enjoyed such romantic overtones tremendously. After the advent of Miss Corruthers' book, many other little items, cards, and books appeared discussing this fragrant language. Listed in the pages to follow are some of the plants and flowers described in these books. Their messages varied a little here and there with personal perspectives, but for the most part the interpretations were consistent so that the scented vocabulary could be ingeniously employed by any who knew it.

The Victorians, besides being a social lot, were also terribly pragmatic in their attitudes. Nothing was wasted, frugality was honored, and creative uses of odd items appeared in every home. Because of this, it would be inappropriate to devise a book on the Victorian language of flowers which restricted its use to simply the creation of an oracle. Instead, for each plant is included a list of the commonly ascribed gender, planet, element, magical associations, and deities.

If you are new to magic, gender refers to masculine or feminine attributes given to the flower hundreds of years ago. Our ancestors felt that all things in nature moved within these boundaries. Frequently the "sex" of the plant was also determined by its predominant element (Earth, Air, Fire, or Water). Besides this information, you will also find a little history and folklore, various magical recipes, and ideas for both practical and metaphysical applications of the various flora. Each chapter will also include some suggestions as to where to find pictures or actual snippets to help you in creating your finished oracle. Please remember that you may combine symbolisms, specifically those of color, runes, and placement, to help enhance the overall effect of your device (see Chapter Seven).

Since many of the recipes shared herein are edible, I would caution readers against using any flowers, leaves, etc. in their preparations which have been treated with pesticides. Organic gardening may be a little more difficult, but the chemical ingredients in most commercially produced bug repellents can be harmful to your health. Likewise, I really feel that natural ingredients overall are best for any type of successful magical working.

If you do choose to try some of the preparations, which I hope you will, remember that even modest cooking skills can be transformed into a magical experience simply by adding a visualization, chant, or even a little song. I remember as a child my grandmother would often hum a tune in the kitchen while she baked. To this day, I believe her love filled that song, and the food she created through that joyful energy. You could actually *feel* it while you ate!

In reviewing the list of possible plants and associations for use in this book, the study became almost overwhelming. So, listed herein are only some of the more frequently noted plants and their meanings. The applications for modern magic are certainly not limited to creating your oracle. The following are suggestions for other uses.

- ✣ Add the dried plant to an incense being used for a ritual or spell. For example, add heather to your incense if doing a spell to bring peacefulness to an otherwise harried situation.

- ✣ Add the dried plant to sachets, or make them into anointing oils for magical use. According to the Victorian flower language, a love sachet or perfumed oil might contain myrtle, almond, and clover for love, hope, and luck. Alternatively, an anointing oil for use before divination could be produced from almond, fennel, and yew for awareness, power, and conviction.

- ✣ Our modern world does not always allow us to work during specific moon phases or hours just out of practicality. If you find this is the case in your life, flowers and plants may be picked during those difficult hours on some other convenient day for the effect you need. Just remember to carefully label your containers according to the hour, moon phase, and planetary correspondences for which they were harvested. This way, the plant may then be used in lieu of working at that specific time.

- ✣ Don't be afraid to use other texts to enrich the uses for your flower language. Look up your prospective ingredients in a good herb book. Use them according to their color correspondence and alternative magical associations. To illustrate, if you don't happen to have a red candle for a spell dealing with physical energy, but you *do* have a bright orange marigold, you can use the color of the marigold in place of the candle! (See also "Color" in Chapter Seven.)

- It should be noted that in your divinatory work, you can reverse the direction of the flower (e.g. bloom downward) to transpose the proposed meaning and energy, or break the plant altogether. For example, if you want to stop gossip or back-stabbing towards a specific person, try crushing sweet William during your spell or ritual as a symbol of destroying that negative demeanor.

- Use the plant as part of an herbal pendulum as described previously.

- Add the plant to altar arrangements, circle decorations, or any other creative magical endeavor to allow for greater symbolism. For example, hawthorn is an appropriate flower to decorate the ritual space for handfastings since it is the emblem of joy and a sacred flower of the Goddess.

By applying your herbs and flowers in such creative ways, this book will not become dust-covered after your deck is completed, but can continue to enrich your spells and rites any time you want to use one of the plants described herein. In this way, a little bit of Victorian ingenuity, beauty, and peacefulness can enter your life, not just through your oracle, but through simple magics, born out of the ritual of living, every day.

CHAPTER FOUR

Flowers

To see a World in a Grain of Sand,
And a Heaven in a Wild Flower,
Hold Infinity in the palm of your hand,
And Eternity in an hour.

William Blake

As discussed in Chapter Three, the Victorians were completely enamored with the natural world. But, even more than the beauty of each tree and stone, the simple resplendence of flowers was admired with almost sacred regard. A home void of blossoms seemed out of place during the Victorian age, for even upholstery fabric was created to reflect their petals' gentle gaze into each room. This profound admiration is perhaps best evidenced by the fact that blossoms far outnumber all other natural items listed in the language of flowers (and thus, in this book).

It should be noted in true Victorian manner, that flowers were not simply a decoration or item of fancy, they were also an art form in more ways than you might expect. Besides the flower books spoken of earlier, dried flower arrangements might find their way onto whimsical boxes, wall decorations, and fashion accessories (especially hats). Flowers were also an extremely useful item to the Victorian kitchen for a wide variety of culinary and medicinal applications. Many of these pantry delights are shared in the following pages.

Buttercup

Gender: Masculine
Planet: Sun
Element: Fire
Magical Association:
Youth, energy, innocence,
divination, prosperity

Folklore/History

Many of us as children can remember running up to a friend and placing this little flower beneath his or her chin to see if he or she liked butter. While not much has been written about the buttercup, it is a lovely addition to any flower pressing or spring nosegay, and it certainly elicits warm reminiscings from our youth.

For magic, the buttercup functions well for any spell needing fiery energy to motivate it or rituals pertaining to finding lost items, healing childhood memories, and improving overall financial stability.

Interpretation

Upright: The flower of gold foretells an improvement in your monetary position. A raise may be on its way, or perhaps a gift from a friend or family member. The way the money (or valuable item) comes to you will most likely be a pleasant, quite unexpected surprise; however, a little patience may be called for. Just like its namesake, this flower tantalizes us with a promise, but fate churns slowly until the perfected outcome is manifest.

Reversed: The buttercup warns to take care with finances. Rebalance your checkbook and be leery of non-cash funds from people whom you don't know well. Don't order anything through the mail right now unless it is a reliable source. You may have an unexpected bill come in, or repair work on a major appliance soon, so keep a little nest egg handy just in case. If you plan to invest in an item or stock, it would be good to check it out thoroughly first. Don't trust first impressions; things may not be as they seem.

Personal Notes

Carnation

Gender: Masculine
Planet: Sun
Element: Fire
Magical Association:
Safety, strength, energy, bravery

Folklore/History

Sometimes called gillyflowers, the carnation in Elizabethan times was believed to keep one from death by hanging. Louis II of Bourbon occupied his time in the Bastille cultivating the flowers, therefore they were often worn by his soldiers as a sign of courage.

The dried blossoms are effectively used in sachets and incense. While fresh, the carnation offers a wide variety of culinary treats including vinegar, salads, and jams. To prepare a syrup of carnations, take half a bushel of petals and bruise them, making sure no seeds or whites are left in the pot. Add one quart of water and bring to just below the boiling point. Let this mixture stand overnight. Now mix in four pounds of sugar and let set another twenty-four hours. Boil until thickened, strain, and jar.

Interpretation

Upright: A flower which indicates admiration, but usually that of business or friendly acquaintances. Your graciousness and courtesy builds others' opinions of you and may eventually lead to positive improvements on the home or office fronts if you're consistent. Don't be afraid to lean heavily on your instincts right now and speak your mind in clear, defined terms. People are listening with refreshed appreciation.

In this position the carnation can also portend social occasions of a festive nature. An invitation to a formal or costume ball, wedding, cocktail party, or other gathering of friends may soon arrive!

Reversed: This card indicates a falling out of favor with someone you know. There may be a minor tiff, clash of opinion on technicalities, or other irritations that cause a temporary but very angry separation. In some respects, this is healthy, like a housecleaning where you air out the grievances to let in a new wind. With a little time and patience the relationship should heal, and may even be better for the candid discourse.

Personal Notes

Chrysanthemum

Gender: Male
Planet: Sun
Element: Fire
Magical Association:
Protection, survival, humor

Folklore/History

The Chinese believe that eating chrysanthemums will increase your longevity, and it makes a good culinary flower for teas, wines, oils, and salads. To make a salad to protect yourself and improve your disposition, take the petals of ten flowers and wash them well. Blanch quickly with salt water then add some cooked potatoes, shrimp, a hint of vinegar, chopped hard-boiled egg, and pepper. Chill and serve with a smile!

Interpretation

Upright: In the Victorian flower language the chrysanthemum can indicate a life of ease, but not one which comes because it is handed to you on a silver platter. Instead, this flower signifies repose for which you have worked. A time of adversity is coming to an end; a time when your own sense of humor has been your greatest ally. Don't lose it now just as the clouds are about to clear. Keep smiling! Soon there will be something very real for which you should be happy. It may not be grand or fancy, but will warm your heart and renew your faith.

Reversed: This card portends a period of hardship on the horizon. Somehow you have lost your perspective and may have made a bad decision based on an emotional whim instead of thoughtful insight. Unfortunately, it is too late to retract the action or decision. You can, however, meet the days ahead with the knowledge that the future is not carved in stone. You have the power to turn a seemingly minor disaster into a positive situation if you can keep mirth in your back pocket and recognize that all mistakes offer the opportunity to learn.

Personal Notes

Clover

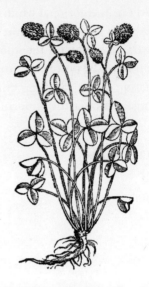

Gender: Male
Planet: Mercury
Element: Air
Magical Association:
Success, love, protection
(white), finances (red), luck

Folklore/History

Wild clover can be made into cordials and vinegar, the seeds and dried flowers are used in Scotland to make bread, and historically clover was often used in baths with mallow, chamomile flowers, and milk to soothe melancholy.

To prepare a type of honey which can be shared with a friend or loved one to inspire improved affections, take five cups of sugar, one and one-quarter cups water, and one teaspoon alum and boil together until clear. Pour this mixture over thirty-six clover buds and four rose buds. Let stand for ten minutes, strain, and bottle. This is especially nice with scones, toast, or as a bread glaze.

Interpretation

Upright: Fate has smiled on you and your life is (or soon will be) filled with fruitful efforts. Whatever media is best for you, use it now with new success. This is a creative card, and may even indicate a pregnancy on a biological level. Emotionally, you are feeling positive, fertile with ideas, and have energy to spare. Spiritual growth is escalating in ways you never dreamed possible. Enjoy this time, like you would the first warm day of spring. Let it refresh your soul.

Reversed: This card may indicate a frustrating run of seemingly bad luck or awkward circumstances. Writer's block or other similar artistic obstructions occur. While only transient in nature, it is very disheartening to the point where all attempts at originality seem to fail. The only really good news is that something positive *will* come out of the whole mess even if it is not immediately recognizable. It may be that you need to try a different avenue or are knocking on the wrong doors. For now, take a deep breath and try and get alternative perspectives.

Personal Notes

Cowslip

Gender: Female
Planet: Venus
Element: Water
Magical Association:
Healing, youthful perspective,
treasure finding, lost items

Folklore/History

Cowslip is sometimes known as a "faerie cup" because of its appearance and its sacredness to the goddess Freya. The old Saxon name for the flower is *cusluppe*. Cowslip can be used in butter, salads, vinegars, mead, pudding, and cake.

A very nice recipe to which a little magic can be added is a cordial to aid sleep and bring renewed energy. For this, combine one quart of wine with a handful of cowslip flowers, a handful of borage petals, and a sprig of rosemary. Set this on your fire until it almost burns. Then add a dash of clove and rose or carnation water. Take one small glassful before bedtime or prior to performing any ritual or spell for health and vitality. (Be sure to strain the mixture before imbibing.) Alternatively, as a libation for success, sprinkle a little on the ground near the area where you want to find a lost object.

Interpretation

Upright: The upright cowslip is an indication of pensiveness. You are going around in circles about a particular matter, but the struggle is not with others, it's with yourself. Thought and consideration are important to decisions, but the counsel of this card is to take care you don't become morose and actually obstructed by your intense deliberation. In this position, the cowslip can also be a sign of the faerie folk's activity in your life. Perhaps things have been moved around, or disappeared altogether, and it's left you scratching your head. Try leaving a small thimble of cream or some honey where they can find it, and see if the trickery stops.

Reversed: Carefree and lively, the reversed cowslip is like the saucer of milk overturned by a kitten. You are happy about the resulting treat, but oh, what a mess! Somehow frivolity has landed you in a situation which is almost a comedy of errors. Yet, despite the difficulties, something pleasurable is also happening. An example might be that in a moment of fun, you end up with green hair from helping a friend paint his or her house. The cowslip's advice, no matter the situation, is to laugh and enjoy the moment for what it is. Drink your fill of cream, then clean it up.

Personal Notes

Daisy

Gender: Male
Planet: Sun
Element: Fire
Magical Association:
Protection, survival, humor

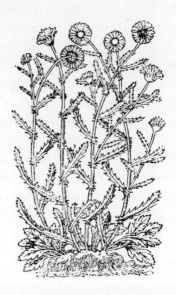

Folklore/History

The daisy, a simple but beautiful flower, has several applications in the culinary arts, specifically making wine. In the fifteenth century, daisies were very popular for salads and were called "day's eye." There is an old saying which tells us if you step on seven daisies at the same time, you know that summer has come!

For magic, the daisy offers a wide variety of creative uses. In spring, the daisy is a welcome addition to decorate an altar or signify the southern portion of the circle. In summer, the blossoms may be twined together to join a handfasted couple. Dried daisy might do well in any incense which is used to lighten the atmosphere of your home and bring improved temperament.

Interpretation

Upright: The daisy is the symbol of the child within and the purity of love. Drawing this card may indicate the beginning of a playful, healthy relationship, be it between lovers or companions. It may also indicate a reconnection in your life with the spirit of simplicity that filled youthful eyes. Make some time in your schedule to visit dear friends and have a picnic in the country. This is a wonderful opportunity to rediscover the world anew from mud pies and romps in the woods to quiet rest beneath a tree, so enjoy it! Also, because of the daisy's association with love magic and divination, you may discover new spiritual or psychic talents manifesting along these lines. Try to be open and learn to use your gifts with appropriate respect.

Reversed: This card indicates a need in your life for some old-fashioned R and R. You have gotten caught up in the web of 101 projects or an old routine and are not giving yourself enough "down time." In some ways you may feel tired of always having to be the adult in a specific situation and are yearning to break free, but a sense of responsibility holds you back. Remember that helping people is fine, living for someone else is not. Everyone has to find his or her own way, including you. Set down the part of you trying to be a messiah and realize that without laughter, rest, and care of the self, you can't help anyone.

Personal Notes

Dandelion

Gender: Male
Planet: Jupiter
Element: Air
Magical Association:
Ancient oracles, wish magic,
communication

Folklore/History

Culpeper believed that the dandelion, a native of Greece, made an excellent herb bath, and Hecate was said to have once entertained Theseus with dandelion wine. This scourge of our yards is also high in vitamins B and C, and may be made into beer, omelets, soups, salads, etc. The fresh juice of the dandelion is a handy remedy for itchy insect bites.

Its leaves may be steeped to create an iced tea, and a special coffee, excellent for the organs, can be made from dandelion root. Begin by cleaning the roots thoroughly then allowing to dry. Brown them in the oven and store in an airtight container. Grind as you would any coffee. The added advantage to this is that it is caffeine free.

Interpretation

Upright: Release dandelion seeds and they will tell you which way the wind blows. Because of this the dandelion is an oracle or messenger to your door. Something is just around the corner, but much depends on the whims of fate. There is a feeling of uncertainty, restlessness which you can't seem to shake. You may not be sleeping well or find yourself fidgety without any visible cause.

Reversed: Unless you decide to include your own alternative interpretation (see Chapter One), the dandelion has no reversed position, so it can portend good or ill from the events or individuals soon to be evidenced to explain this sensation. The dandelion's message? Be prepared for a gust.

Personal Notes

Foxglove

Gender: Feminine
Planet: Venus
Element: Water
Magical Association:
Protection

Folklore/History

Foxglove is also known as "folk's gloves" because of its association with the
faeries. It has tubular lavender flowers, and presently is one of the major
sources of natural digitalis for heart conditions.

The plant can grow up to six feet tall, and therefore is an excellent
companion for walls and background decoration in a garden. It will grow
in a wide range of soil, and may be used with alum to make a chartreuse
colored dye. Generally, the foxglove is not good to use in home herbal
preparations because of the toxicity caused by improper measurements.

Interpretation

Upright: The flower of our ambitions, drawing the foxglove indicates
that something we have earnestly worked for is close to attainment. Very
often this plant also indicates the passing of a certain "gestation" period,
often just over a year, where the objective was developed and strived for.
This is the harvest of labors well planted and tended. In relationships, it
may well indicate a marriage which will be long-lasting. In business, a

contract or promotion may be at hand. On the personal level, it is often an indicator that the individual's voice in a particular artistic medium has been found and appreciated by others.

Reversed: The foxglove warns that nothing good will come of being overly ambitious, greedy, or having bad intentions in your personal projects. Do not try to rush or take shortcuts with what must often be a slow growing process. Narrow down the focus of your dreams and visions to those which really inspire you to do and be your best, and which you can realistically strive for. Double-check your motivations for any planned activities to be sure your heart is in the right place.

Personal Notes

Geranium

Gender: Feminine
Planet: Venus
Element: Water
Magical Association:
Fertility, health, protection;
red flowers signify guests and
pink petals signify love

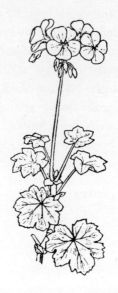

Folklore/History

There is a story which tells us that the geranium was born when the prophet Mahomet's shirt was tossed over a mallow plant to dry in the sun. With this in mind, it is not surprising to discover that the geranium has its beginnings in the East.

To make a rose geranium punch, which is terrific for summer rites and any festivals of love, take one quart of apple juice, the petals from six rose geraniums, and one cup of sugar and mix over a low flame until it boils for five minutes. Add four crushed limes, then cool and strain. You may garnish each ritual cup with a few blossoms.

Interpretation

Upright: Geranium is the flower of remembrance. In this instance it indicates some type of reunion. An old acquaintance may suddenly come back into your life now, and with him or her comes a flood of memories (both good and bad). The past can be a welcome friend or a haunting ghost; but either way, greet the moment. Somewhere in this happenstance is an opportunity for something more. Remember that the web of life is always expanding outward, and this encounter is part of that connection.

The geranium also reminds us that our past is part of what has made our today, and not to despise it. Valuable lessons have been learned over time, and while some are painful, they have helped to guide you on your Path. We need to look upon our yesterdays with proper perspective, and be thankful for what they have built in us

Reversed: This flower is a warning that you may be living too much in the past and letting the "here and now" pass you by. Sometimes the greatest gift we can give an individual or situation is to let it fly free, instead of flaunting the memory like a badge of honor. Leave the past where it belongs, and turn your eyes forward to building a future.

Personal Notes

Hollyhock

Gender: Feminine
Planet: Venus
Element: Water
Magical Association:
Success, money, flourishing
family, friendship to the faeries

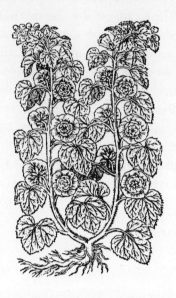

Folklore/History

The hollyhock has been a part of Chinese cooking for thousands of years because of its rich nutrient content. The fresh buds and petals are put into salads, the stalks may be cooked and used as a side dish, and a combination of both, with a little lemon verbena and marigold, can be served as a meal in itself.

In the late 1600s a Reverend Friend wrote a recipe which incorporated hollyhocks as a means to see faeries. A slightly revised version of this preparation uses one pint of salad oil, rose and marigold water from flowers gathered in the east, buds of hollyhock, thyme, hazel, and marigolds plucked from near a faerie hill, and a sprig of grass from the knoll itself. Set all of the ingredients in the sun for three days, strain, and then apply the oil to the eyelids for enhanced Sight.

Interpretation

Upright: Hollyhock indicates you have made (or will be making) some excellent decisions based on preparedness and ambition fulfilled. Rely heavily on your ability to plan, organize, and keep a healthy perspective now. Mental fortitude will bring a reasonable amount of success in almost any endeavor. So much so that this card may indicate a promotion or other positive news which fosters "good wishes" and celebratory moods from those around you.

Reversed: Hollyhock speaks of a lack of foresight, procrastination, and avoidance of responsibility. These types of actions may lead you to difficulties designed by fate specifically to wake you up. As a wise person once said, when you try to run from something, more often than not you end up dashing headlong into it.

Along the same lines, the inverted hollyhock can also warn of ineffectual or misunderstood communications. Here, your quick tongue may have become your own enemy, to be swiftly harnessed before worse trouble results. Give a little more thought to the way you phrase things before blurting them out. In this case, the hollyhock advises that diplomacy, sensitivity, and consideration are called for in any discourse.

Personal Notes

Honeysuckle

Gender: Male
Planet: Jupiter
Element: Earth
Magical Association:
Protection, psychic vision,
financial matters

Folklore/History

The honeysuckle has been most revered for its innate ability to grow in a wide variety of conditions, even after being cut severely back. Magically, it is an excellent component for any spell or ritual where you wish to improve your understanding of reality beyond the normal range of senses.

A lovely syrup can be made from the petals of this flower. To prepare, take two pounds of petals and four pints of water and infuse them for twelve hours. Press slightly, setting aside only the liquor. Strain this thoroughly, adding twice as much sugar as liquid, and warming it on the stove until it becomes thick. Store in an airtight container.

Honeysuckle wine, good for summer festivals, is made by bringing one gallon each of flowers and water to a low rolling boil. Add to this two and a half pounds of sugar or honey, one sliced lemon and orange, and a piece of bruised ginger root. Half a package of yeast suspended in one-quarter cup of water should be added when the mixture is lukewarm. Allow this to ferment in a stoneware pot for two weeks, cover with a towel, then strain into bottles corked loosely for two months before sealing.

Interpretation

Upright: The sweetness of this flower's nectar is in the attributes of fidelity, honesty, and integrity. When it appears in a spread you can rest assured that you have dealt fairly with a person or situation which has nagged at your heart. This card speaks of an inner peacefulness. No matter what others may think or perceive, you truly have acted in good faith to the best of your ability. Stop browbeating yourself, and trust in your heart. Within a few weeks things will blow over, and you will still be left knowing you have followed your conscience.

Reversed: The honeysuckle warns that things are not always as they seem. Someone near you is not being completely honest in their dealings with you, especially in matters of finance or love. The advice here is to not automatically accept excuses or explanations at face value, but proceed carefully, trying to weed out any deception as you go. The individual involved may be acting under misinformation or false pretenses, so don't judge him or her too harshly until your facts are in.

Personal Notes

Hyacinth

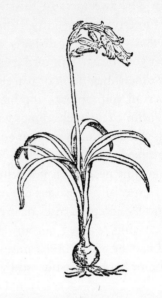

Gender: Feminine
Planet: Venus
Element: Water
Magical Association:
Love, mirth, protection

Folklore/History

Greek legends claim that Apollo made this flower as part of one of the great myth cycles traditional to that culture. Interestingly enough, a popular dish on the Isle of Crete is still grape hyacinth pickles.

Magically the hyacinth may be used to ward against nightmares, relieve depression, and improve mental concentration, especially if prepared as an incense. Another fun use is the preparation of a spring wine in which these blossoms, violets, orange flowers, jonquils, marigolds, and any other edible flowers of the season are warmed in a gallon of fine wine. The flowers simply lend their fresh scent to the drink, which can then be bottled or served immediately.

Interpretation

Upright: The Victorians perceived this as a flower of reliability and enjoyment. In this case, the pleasure has come from your own sense of continuity and the ability to finish what you start. You may have completed a major project early, or gotten paid for an endeavor, leaving you with a little free time and extra funds to spoil yourself. The advice of this card is to do just that. Go somewhere you have always wanted to go, or just treat yourself to some ice cream. Enjoy the opportunity to reward yourself for a job well done.

Reversed: Procrastination, distraction, and frustration seem to be prevalent in your actions and mood. You may feel as if you have accomplished nothing productive in a long time, and suddenly realize most of the problem is due to stalling, excuses, and a general lack of ambition.

You need to find something to really focus your attention on, which will also help motivate you towards the best effort you can give. Discover that one thing, following it through to the end with determination, and you will also discover a new sense of self.

Personal Notes

Iris

Gender: Feminine
Planet: Venus
Element: Water
Magical Association:
Wisdom, purification,
protection, romance

Folklore/History

Iris is the goddess of the rainbow. This flower is not only associated with her, but also Hera, Isis, and Juno. The three petals of the iris are believed by some to represent either the threefold nature of the Goddess herself or the attributes of bravery, discernment, and faith. In Roman times, these blossoms were dispersed in any room where purification and cleansing was desired.

Medicinally, the powdered root is sometimes used as an infusion for gas, coughs, and swollen glands. Externally as a poultice, it helps relieve the discomfort of bites and stings. More commonly known as orrisroot, this is one of the best fixatives for incense preparations.

Interpretation

Upright: In the heart of this flower is promise—promise of a better tomorrow, promises made and kept, promise that your efforts mean something. This is a pledge from the universe that you will not be forgotten in the greater scheme, but that your life is important. Because of the hopeful nature of this flower, an advantageous proposal, especially of a personal nature, may soon follow. Tensions are easing now, and you will find you have fresher perspectives and revitalized energy.

If the iris appears upright in your spread when you are about to enter into a long-term relationship, it is extremely positive. This indicates a strong karmic connection and sense of fidelity which will be lasting.

Reversed: The iris warns of making too many commitments which you may not be able to keep. It also cautions you against holding high expectations from others' assurances to you. Certain deals you thought were solid may fall through or prove undependable at best. Read the fine print on contracts, don't spread yourself too thin, and discard your rose-colored glasses, especially with regards to a relationship.

Personal Notes

Jasmine

Gender: Feminine
Planet: Moon
Element: Water
Magical Association:
Prophetic dreams, love,
money, maternal aspects,
psychic protection

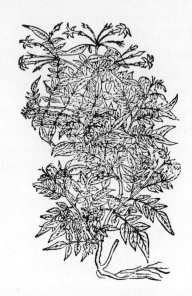

Folklore/History

The jasmine has found its way into the lore of several deities including Vishnu, Kwan Yin, and Diana. The culinary delights of this flower are by no means limited. Besides liquors, fondants, cakes, scented water, and syrup, the petals can be used to scent tea (one pound of tea to one-third pound of flowers are the proportions used in Eastern lands).

To internalize any of the magical aspects of jasmine in a tasty way, take one cup of applesauce and one pound of jasmine petals, mixing until smooth. Next, bring two cups of water and one pound of sugar to a boil until they reach hard-crack stage for candy. Add your flower mix at this point, boiling for ten minutes more, then pour on a well-greased cookie sheet and place in a warm oven to dry. Crack apart and eat!

Interpretation

Upright: A flower of the Orient, this card is one of favorable mystery. Something odd may happen which leaves you scratching your head, but when you discover the answer it will be a pleasant surprise. This card may portend an anonymous gift or admirer, new friendships from unexpected situations, spontaneous lunches with coworkers, and other enjoyable activities of an unplanned nature.

This card also indicates a new charisma developing in your life. You will naturally begin to draw friends, students, or other fresh acquaintances into your life by your renewed spiritual "fragrance." Internal changes are manifesting themselves outwardly with positive results!

Reversed: The jasmine warns to be leery of anything which seems too good to be true. Don't trust the mysterious stranger or generous offer which crosses your path without serious scrutiny. Likewise, in your spiritual life, be cautious of what you accept as "truth." Do not allow someone else to become an undisputed guru for your spiritual quest, no matter how alluring he or she may be. Teachers and spirit guides have limited knowledge. You must depend on your own sensibilities to know if this knowledge should be applied in your life.

Personal Notes

Lavender

Gender: Male
Planet: Mercury
Element: Air
Magical Association:
Sleep (incense), chastity, pure
joy and love, peacefulness

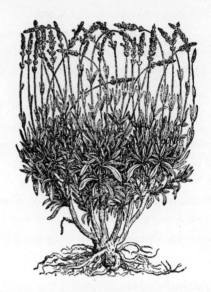

Folklore/History

From Roman times until the present, lavender has been a favored flower to place in sweetbags for baths, chests, and cupboards because of its light scent and mild ability to repel insects. Another early custom was to wear sprigs of lavender stuffed in a hat to protect yourself from getting head colds.

Like many other flowers listed herein, lavender is also edible and can be made into wine and teas. A nice way to dry this plant is to tie sprigs of it to strings and hang them in your windows. Not only will you have lavender to use year-round, but your house will smell lovely as well.

Interpretation

Upright: The answer to a question or resolution to a situation long on your heart is right around the corner, so don't despair. When given, lavender requests a response; when received, *it is* the response. Be it a personal or professional matter, the reply to your inquiry will turn out to be right under your nose and easily obtained. Actually, it may turn out that you have been so worried as to have missed it altogether up until now. Either way, it will come as a welcome, definitive relief to the uncertainty you have been experiencing.

Reversed: This card may indicate an untimely delay to an answer or, worse yet, a response you did not want to hear. The delay or negativity here is not of your doing, but must be handled in a positive manner if any good is to come. The advice here is to not make assumptions or allow your fears or concern to overwhelm you. Things can still work out in your favor.

Personal Notes

Lemon Blossom

Gender: Feminine
Planet: Venus/Moon
Element: Water
Magical Association:
Friendship, love, purification,
long life

Folklore/History

Lemon blossoms are a nice addition to spring water for cleansing your magical tools. The petals are also used for scenting butter, tarts, puddings, and fritters.

To make a refreshing ice cream out of lemon blossom, take one pint of heavy cream and one-quarter teaspoon of salt and scald them quickly over a flame. Pour this mixture over eight slightly beaten egg yolks, stirring constantly, while adding two ounces of the ground flowers and half a cup of sugar. Cook this in a double boiler until it thickens. Strain, cool, and pour into a pan to freeze. Serve to a dear friend visiting on a hot summer's day!

Interpretation

Upright: A situation has come up where you are being called on to remain discrete and trustworthy, which will not necessarily be simple. You may be getting different stories and signals from people which make no sense, and feel as if your tolerance for gossip is being stretched to its limit.

The suggestion of this card is to do your best to prevail. For some reason, people are looking to you for an impartial, well-balanced viewpoint. You must trust in your instincts and ability to "sniff out" the truth from several different versions presented in order to find a solution which is fair to everyone.

Reversed: This card speaks of a time when your modesty and judgment are definitely in question. The voices of people around you seem critical and hesitant. A certain sense of trust has been lost. While it may not have been intentional on your part, you have somehow broken a confidence and it desperately needs to be mended; not only for the sake of your reputation but also to heal the rifts forming between you and your friends. Take the time to listen to their words and viewpoints with an open heart.

Personal Notes

Lilac

Gender: Feminine
Planet: Venus
Element: Water
Magical Association:
Banishing negativity,
protection, releasing spirits

Folklore/History

A native of Asia Minor, the lilac (its Persian name is *lilak*) first appeared
in France in 1597. In Russia, the flowers are used to make a special linea-
ment for rheumatism. More frequently, though, the petals are employed
in candy novelties such as flavoring marzipan.

My personal favorite use for lilacs is in making scented oil which can
be applied for meditation or just enjoyment. Begin with two cups of
sesame or almond oil which has been warmed and placed in a dark bottle.
To this add two handfuls of petals only. Allow the petals to steep in a
sunny place until they become almost transparent. Repeat as often as necessary to reach the desired strength.

Interpretation

Upright: Lilac is the flower of our first, innocent love. This love can be
towards a person or an art, but it is very real, deep, abiding, and will
change the way you view the world around you. There is an excitement
which flows from your heart; you want to dance or jump for the sheer joy

of it. Like a dolphin breaking the water, you are flying emotionally and have seemingly endless energy. However, the initial force of new projects will eventually ease off to a steadier pace, so try and keep one foot on the ground. This way when you land, you are ready to keep walking!

Reversed: This card indicates that this new passion may consume your time and seize all of your attention before you even become aware of it. Take care however, that it does not do so at the expense of other equally important matters. The fires of love must be evenly fed, not burning out of control, if they are to last.

Personal Notes

Lily

Gender: Feminine
Planet: Moon
Element: Water
Magical Association:
Divine knowledge, breaking
love, solving crimes, purity,
quests

Folklore/History

The lily seems to be an integral part of many allegories in Egyptian and
Hebrew lore. The Greeks call it the flower of flowers, and the Christian
tradition even likens it to the beauty of Christ. Other deities associated
with the lily are Venus, Kwan Yin, and Juno. Also, you can burn dried lily
in appeasement to your kitchen god as they do in China.

Lilies are used frequently in Asian cultures to flavor chicken, rice,
soup, noodles, pork, and fish. A sauce for this type of preparation is usually made with three-fourths cup of petals and a dash of soy sauce and
sherry. The lily bulb can be used similarly. Medicinally, the petals can be
made into a poultice with mild antiseptic value.

Interpretation

Upright: Lily is a blossom of purity, especially with respect to the emotions. If love comes to you now, it will be true. There is new uniformity
and clarity to your spiritual quest which is likewise manifesting in your
daily life. You are learning to master your emotions, balancing the heart

and head into a effective mechanism for magic and life. This is a time when simple pleasures will be most enjoyed; a roaring fire, good friends, quiet music. Like the pieces of a puzzle, your life will begin to fall into place.

Reversed: The lily indicates a great deal of confusion, usually of an emotional nature. You may have recently experienced an argument or separation from a friend, a divorce, an unexpected move, or other upheaval which has left your life seemingly in suspense. In this instance, the drastic change was necessary to help redirect your focus. Somehow this circumstance came about due to neglect of something which was important for you to do. The lily reminds us that when there is no wind to move the boat, you must row. When there are no paddles, use your hands. Do not become stagnant now. Get creative!

Personal Notes

Lotus

Gender: Feminine
Planet: Moon
Element: Water
Magical Association:
Surety of spiritual energy, the
ability to know when to act,
opening doors, protection

Folklore/History

In Eastern countries, the lotus is the symbol of life itself; past, present, and future. It may have been because of this association that the Egyptians offered this flower to their gods. Osiris and Hermes are among the deities associated with the lotus.

In China, the lotus tubers are candied or eaten as a vegetable, the stems are dried to make arrowroot, the kernels become soups, and the seeds are prepared for teas. Similarly in Japan, lotus pudding and flavored rice can be found. To make your own lotus soup, put six cups of chopped root (soak for several hours before chopping to tenderize), a bit of ginger, shredded tangerine rind, two cups of chicken, soy, and garlic in boiling water. Add extra items and seasonings to taste.

Interpretation

Upright: Authenticity of word and deed, purity of heart and intention. This is a card, when it appears in the outcome position of any spread, which says, "You have done well." No matter what the circumstances have been, you have stayed true to your ideals and Path, refusing to be hypo-critical. While the rewards for this diligence may not be seen on the material level (indeed, in some cases integrity can be costly), spiritually you will reap a harvest uncommon to most people in a lifetime.

Reversed: A warning not to give in to a proposal which seems morally, emotionally, or physically inappropriate to you. No matter how tempting this offer may seem, answering it would leave you with many regrets and possibly some heart-rending scars. Stay true to your own sensibilities.

Personal Notes

Marigold

Gender: Male
Planet: Sun
Element: Fire
Magical Association:
Protection, legal matters,
psychic dreams, garlands for
respect; if picked at noon, the
marigold can strengthen or
comfort an ailing heart

Folklore/History

The marigold has become an important homeopathic cure internally for flu, fever, gas, and painful menstruation. Externally, a lotion or compress of the flower will produce a salve for itching and wounds. A tea of the petals makes a good hair rinse to bring out highlights.

In England and Germany marigolds are used extensively in the kitchen for flavoring eggs, soups, cheese, rice, and even sliced onto liverwurst sandwiches. If you would like to make some biscuits, appropriate for fire festivals, mix together one cup of flour, three ounces of lard, three ounces of butter, one teaspoon of baking powder, one-quarter cup of sugar, and a pinch of salt. Chop up some red or yellow fruits to add as well. In the meantime, soak a handful of marigolds in a cup of hot milk. Cool and blend in a beaten egg, then add this mixture to the dry blend. Stir well and bake at 350° for about fifteen minutes until golden brown. Garnish with marigolds.

Interpretation

Upright: The marigold is a flower of hardship, misfortune, and sorrow. It may indicate the passing of a friend or beloved animal, a broken relationship, or other misadventures which either discourage you or leave you feeling defeated. In every life there are periodic refining fires to endure, and this is a hot one, but you can make it with the help of friends and humor as a bedfellow. Your worst enemy right now might not be the problems, but your pride. Don't feel awkward about reaching out for a little support and comfort until the storm is past.

    Reversed: The marigold is a sign that a time of mourning or difficulty is coming to an end, and a new day is dawning. You may feel as if you have awakened from a long sleep, with some dismay as to how long it's been since you've seen such a glorious sunrise, but rejoice! The night is over. The tears you have cried were ones of cleansing. There are no shadows here to haunt you; you have released them and found new freedom. Now is the time to really live!

Personal Notes

Nasturtium

Gender: Feminine
Planet: Neptune
Element: Air
Magical Association:
Convictions, aspiration,
festivity

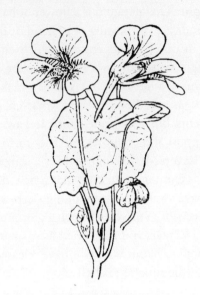

Folklore/History

The nasturtium was originally brought from Peru by Spanish conquistadors in the sixteenth century; its name derives from the Latin *nasus turtus* which means "convulsed noise." The nasturtium has a peppy taste which quickly became popular in Spain for salads, vinegars, and many other dishes, the additional bonus being its high quantity of vitamin C.

To make a sauce which can be used to flavor meats or salads, take one quart of the flowers, one quart of vinegar, six shallots, six cloves, salt and pepper and boil slowly. Keep in a covered jar for one month, then strain and add soy sauce to taste. Another good snack can be made by stuffing large nasturtium petals with tuna salad then sprinkling with a bit of your favorite vinegar.

Interpretation

Upright: This is the card of citizenship and community spirit. An opportunity is being presented to you to get involved and really make a difference where you live. It may seem to be only a minor matter on the surface, but without willing, able hands, nothing can be accomplished. Start a recycling drive, join the PTA, or spend a day picking up litter in a nearby park. Take the opening being offered as a way to quietly allow your magical energy to move out from your home into your town or city, even in small ways.

Reversed: The nasturtium is an indication that you spend an awful lot of time complaining, and very little time doing. Whatever the cause, you tend to expect someone else to handle the bulk of responsibility, even for community projects you may have instigated. The nasturtium is trying to suggest that you not start anything you can't, or are unwilling to, finish completely. It is also a gentle reminder that the welfare of your neighborhood is *everyone's* responsibility, including yours.

Personal Notes

Orange Blossom

Gender: Male
Planet: Sun
Element: Fire
Magical Association:
Divination, love, good fortune,
virtue

Folklore/History

Originally from central Asia, then brought to the Mediterranean, the orange blossom was for a long time a symbol of virginity in brides. From the Middle Ages to the Victorian era, orange blossom water scented the rooms of young women to ease depression and almost every form of "feminine malaise." The petals also were made into wine, brandy, ice cream, honey, jelly, and meringues. Queen Victoria herself loved cream which was perfumed with orange blossoms.

In magic, orange flowers are good for love sachets, and you may bathe in the petals to help beautify your skin. In terms of culinary arts, orange blossoms seem second only to roses in popularity. Orange pekoe tea is still made by scenting black tea with these flowers. Pralines can be prepared by boiling corn syrup to the hard-ball stage, adding a pint of fresh orange flowers off the stalks, boiling until well coated, then rubbing with fine sugar and drying. These will last almost forever!

An orange candy can be made from two cups of sugar and one cup of water boiled until it forms a syrup. To this add almonds, a bit of grated lemon, chunks of dried pineapple, and half a cup of orange blossoms. Pour into a greased pan to set until hardened, then cut into squares.

Interpretation

Upright: The orange blossom is the flower of purity: pure love, pure joy, pure intentions. If someone has been heaping vast amounts of attention on you, and you wondered if it was sincere, the answer is yes. There is no questioning the earnestness of his or her purpose any longer. Actually what you may question more is how you really feel about this attention. Up to now your focus has been so much on doubting that you haven't given yourself the opportunity to decide if it's desired or not. Now is definitely the time to make that choice.

Reversed: Someone seems too good to be true, have too smooth a line, or be presenting an opportunity that is unbelievable. Be leery and forewarned. Honey can be sweet, but it can also make you sick if you swallow too much of it. Try to maintain a well-balanced perspective and not get stuck in this flamboyant web. If you think there is cause for concern, there probably is, so investigate alternative avenues and check references thoroughly before proceeding.

Personal Notes

Orchid

Gender: Androgenous
(see below)
Planet: Venus
Element: Water
Magical Association:
Balance of male-female energy,
love, vision, kinship

Folklore/History

According to legend, the orchid is the favored food of satyrs, possibly because its name derives from the Greek word *orkhis*, meaning testicles. The Chinese consider friendship as bearing the fragrance of orchids. This flower is rather unique because it has both male and female characteristics in the same plant. Because of this it can act as an excellent scent to help balance your personal sexual energies.

In the eighteenth century it was very fashionable to eat orchids, and they are high in nutritional value. You may add petals to a sandwich or make a soup by placing one teaspoon of the powdered root in a pint of water with a touch of wine and lemon juice.

Interpretation

Upright: A flower which symbolizes the perfection of humanity, this card appearing upright in your spread indicates a drastic change in spiritual understanding and insight. Rather like the proverbial light going on over your head, suddenly many things which have alluded you before are now making sense. The order of your life and energy is beginning to flow with that of the universe. You sense a new oneness and synchronization with magical power which can continue to grow if properly tended. This growth is but one step on a long road. Continue to walk it respectfully.

Reversed: A warning that you may be taking your spiritual nature for granted. Study, meditation, and consistency of practice in magical arts is necessary to achieve solid, positive results. Don't expect the universe to answer your needs if you have not expressed them, or made an honest attempt to fulfill them yourself. Get back into a daily routine of tending to the whole person—body, mind, and soul—to get your life back in balance.

Personal Notes

Pansy

Gender: Feminine
Planet: Saturn
Element: Water
Magical Association:
Weather magic, divination, love

Folklore/History

The pansy carries the ancient folk name of "banewort" perhaps because it seems almost antisocial in its growing habits. This wild flower is happiest in sandy soil or high on a hillside. In decoction or compress form it is a good treatment for eczema, psoriasis, and rheumatic pain.

For a little bit of edible floral fun, place whole pansy buds face down in your next Jell-O® mold so guests can find their smiling faces looking up at them!

Interpretation

Upright: The pansy embodies the attributes of consideration, chivalry, and courtesy. While you may feel stretched to your limit, keep these virtues close to you, guarding your words and deeds like a devoted friend.

As tempting as it might be just to blurt out exactly how you feel, nothing good would come of such a display other than your own embarrassment. By maintaining a more professional demeanor, you gain the respect of others and keep your own self-esteem well intact.

Reversed: The overturned pansy is a sign of insensitivity, usually toward someone close by. No matter how many times he or she may have "cried wolf," this plea for assistance is genuine and needs your careful attention. Remaining aloof will do more harm than good right now, and you will eventually regret your inaction. Take the chance and reach out. The resulting transformation just might surprise you.

Personal Notes

Peony

Gender: Male
Planet: Sun
Element: Fire
Magical Association:
Banishing negative energy, luck,
temperance

Folklore/History

Also known as the "king's flower," the peony has been used to scent some of China's highest grade teas. Pliny believed it to be one of the oldest known plants, having been mentioned in written records as early as 320 B.C.

Peony kernels can be eaten as a condiment or used to decorate cream much as almonds might. In England, the seeds of the male plant are carried to protect the individual from magic.

Interpretation

Upright: The flower of riches and honor, your ship is finally about to come in. Be it the rewards of hard labor, an emotional reprieve, or an unexpected promotion, somehow everything is about to look much brighter for your future. This is not a temporary change either, but a cycle which will sustain you for some time. Enjoy it, but with great appreciation for the gifts which come your way.

Reversed: The inverted card warns of a time soon to come when you will have to tighten your belt and really be careful with all your worldly goods. The pressures of such constraint can be difficult to bear, so this card also advises you to do your best not to carry your problems with you like a neon sign. This is a temporary setback, which may take longer than some to rectify (usually the span of two to three years), so don't wallow in negativity. Do your best to cope, keeping humor and hope as constant companions, and you will fare this storm very well.

Personal Notes

Primrose

Gender: Female
Planet: Venus
Element: Earth
Magical Association:
Protection, respect, love

Folklore/History

The evening primrose is known to shut with a loud click come the dusk, making it an interesting addition to the magical garden. Most popular for candies and preserves, the young shoots can be soaked in salt water and served with vinaigrette dressing for a salad. Alternatively you can brown them in butter and garnish with a bit of orange juice.

Interpretation

Upright: Coherence, harmony, and consistency are this flower's message. Whatever course you have been following regarding the question at hand, stick to it, never wavering from your vision, goals, or ethics.

In the home, pay special attention to the feelings of others so that the gentle accord of your house may remain at peace.

Reversed: Your lack of dependability is becoming difficult to bear for those around you, and even may bring harm. No matter how good your intentions, don't get distracted right now. Follow through on the promises you make and be candid if you are unable to meet deadlines.

In the home, take care that you are truthful and fair with house-mates. Even little white lies will come back to haunt you if this card has appeared inverted in your spread.

Personal Notes

Rose

Gender: Feminine
Planet: Venus
Element: Water
Magical Association:
Adoration, good fortune,
psychic dreams

Folklore/History

The mystique of the rose has grown over countless generations for the poet, romantic, cook, and healer alike. Originally the rose was believed to have been born of Aphrodite's blood when her foot got stuck by a thorn while aiding Adonis. When visited by Mark Antony, Cleopatra covered her floor with rose petals in order to secure his love. Also associated with the rose are Eros, Cupid, Demeter, and Isis.

For 3,000 years the rose has been venerated as the queen of flowers. There are presently over 10,000 varieties available. This flower not only became adored for its scent and uncommon beauty, but for its wide-ranging uses in the kitchen. Rose hips yield more vitamin C than oranges.

To extract oil of roses, steep your petals in warm water until they turn almost clear. Move this container to a cool place (such as your refrigerator). When the mixture is cool, there will be dots of oil floating on the surface. Scoop these off and use to condition and scent the skin. This is often called attar of roses and is one of the most valuable flower substances.

Rose wine is made with three to four quarts of petals, three pounds of sugar, one gallon of water, two oranges, one tea bag, and two-thirds package of yeast. Bring all the ingredients, except the yeast, to a low boil until the petals turn clear. Repeat with more petals for a stronger rosy flavor. Once cool, strain out the petals and add the yeast dissolved in warm water. Allow this to work in a covered container for two weeks, then bottle, waiting three months before sealing.

To make a rose pomander, take equal portions of cinnamon, ginger, rose water, powdered clove, nutmeg, myrrh, dried rose petals, and benzoin and crush them together until well mixed. Add a few drops of pink wax and form it into a ball. Once dry, the pomander can be placed in a drawer, hung in a window, or carried to release its lovely scent.

Interpretation

Upright: For the purpose of your oracle, the color of the rose can be just as important as the blossom itself. Red tends to indicate love and passion which is accepted and returned. Pink signifies the simple pleasures in life, and enjoyment of same. White is clarity of thought and intentions, and yellow is an achievement leading to mirth and celebration.

Reversed: Red would be a sign of love gone astray and probably angry tempers. Pink would encourage you not to thirst for other pastures because they need mowing too. White portends that someone is not being totally honest in their dealings with you, therefore caution is urged. Finally, yellow would indicate something you perceive as a failure.

No matter the color, this card reminds you to look at the beauty which is constantly around you before wallowing in anger or pity. There is much good to be found, and frequently it is right under your nose!

Personal Notes

Snapdragon

Gender: Male
Planet: Mars
Element: Fire
Magical Association:
Protection, ward against magic
(seeds)

Folklore/History

For some reason the name of this flower has been given to all manner of food and games, even when there are no snapdragons in the list of ingredients. One recipe called "snapdragons" is made with raisins soaked in cognac till plump then added to applesauce and served. Likewise, the traditional Hallows and Yule game of snapdragon is played with raisins in a bowl of brandy which is lit. The guests then eat the raisins while still seemingly on fire! I presume these traditions have come about due to the lore surrounding fire-breathing dragons, from which the snapdragon takes its name.

Magically, this flower can be worn to protect yourself from undesired circumstances or given to a friend to keep him or her safe.

Interpretation

Upright: This card is an admonition not to be overly presumptuous or arrogant in the way you handle the question at hand. You either do not have 100 percent of the truth in this scenario, or may not understand the extenuating proprieties which are very important to proper action on your part. Stop and listen to the voice of reason and experience around you. Someone is offering sound advice which you haven't really been heeding. Instead of moving forward with haste, slow down and realize you still have a lot to learn.

Reversed: Indicates that arrogance or presumption is directed towards you. In this case, your acquaintances are taking a lot for granted, imposing on your hospitality and just making a nuisance of themselves. Put your foot down and lay some ground rules that you are willing to enforce now before you get buried by "good intentions."

Personal Notes

Tansy

Gender: Feminine
Planet: Venus
Element: Water
Magical Association:
Immortality, health

Folklore/History

From a Greek word which translates as meaning timeless, tansy was given to Ganymede to make him immortal; thus, he became the cup bearer to Zeus. During the sixteenth and seventeenth centuries, tansy was popular as a stewing herb to freshen the air, not to mention culinary applications.

Tansy is not used medicinally because of nasty side effects, but the peppery leaves can make a good spice substitute if used with great moderation. A tansy lotion can help ease acne, and if planted with berry bushes, the tansy flowers help keep ants at bay.

To make tansy pancakes, mix four tablespoons of flour with half a pint of cream. To this add four eggs, two ounces of powdered sugar, half a teaspoon of tansy juice, and a dash of nutmeg. Blend for fifteen minutes, then fry in fresh butter and serve with cream or berries.

Interpretation

Upright: The tansy is a declaration of war, hostility, or conflict from someone near you. Uncontrolled and possibly unconsidered anger is being directed your way during an emotional outburst. The advice of the tansy is to not allow yourself to respond in kind. Take the bitter words only at surface value, being that they are spoken in the heat of the moment, and give that individual time and distance to cool off before trying to make peace. For some people, anger acts like a release valve, once the steam is gone, most of the animosity disappears too.

Reversed: The tansy foresees an end to the difficulties. The white flag is being raised and soon a truce which is fair to all parties will be reached. Depending on your question, this could indicate the resolution of a legal matter, end to an argument with a friend, or even a change in work-related matters. No matter the case, however, this is definitely good news.

Personal Notes

Tulip

Gender: Female
Planet: Venus
Element: Earth
Magical Association:
Protection, prosperity, love

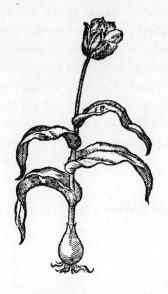

Folklore/History

Once believed to have been in the form of a nymph, the tulip did not really gain any type of recognition until after the 1600s. Later writers such as Sir Kenelm Digby tell us that the seeds when boiled taste much like peas. Persians used the tulip as a declaration of love, Turks have a feast of tulips, and Francis Bacon believed that the opening and closing of this flower at dawn and dusk was to greet and mourn the sun.

For an interesting culinary treat, try removing the petals from a large tulip, washing them, and stuffing with chicken salad.

Interpretation

Upright: In the language of flowers, the tulip reveals that you have beautiful eyes. For our oracle, the eyes are the window to the soul. Your spiritual insight and wisdom are at a high point right now. Use this period for studying your Path and sharing same.

You may also notice that your instinctive sense about new people you meet is heightened, almost to a visual level, regarding their personal energy and intentions. This is for a good reason. Someone may soon come your way presenting themselves falsely. Your penetration of this visage will save you and others much trouble.

Reversed: Do not rely too heavily on your instincts right now. For some reason your reception is cloudy and what you perceive may not be accurate. Perhaps your emotional state is in turmoil or mundane matters have you running hither and yon. Whatever the case, your concentration is definitely suffering. You may need to segregate the different areas of your life a little more to be able to see clearly what you need to do.

Personal Notes

Violet

Gender: Feminine
Planet: Venus
Element: Water
Magical Association:
Humility, insight, calm tempers,
desire, luck, sleep, peace

Folklore/History

When the goddess Io was changed by Zeus into a heifer, he also gave her a pasture of violets to eat. In the days of the troubadour, a golden violet was often given as a prize to the best muse.

Today the violet is valued for its oil which is used in perfume, and the petals are still frequently made into candy, jelly, sauce, vinegars, and salads. Both the blossoms and leaves of this plant are rich in vitamin C. They may also be used in ointments and compresses.

For a more Victorian air, the Queen herself was fond of violet tea with honey (one teaspoon dried leaves to one cup water). She also favored a syrup which was prepared by boiling half a pound of dried petals, one pound of sugar, a bit of orrisroot, one ounce of gum arabic, and half a cup of water. This is wonderful on pancakes and waffles.

Interpretation

Upright: Your steadfast, faithful efforts are about to be rewarded. Whatever you have been striving for will soon begin to materialize, much to your pleasant surprise. For a writer, this might portend a publishing contract, for the student, a scholarship, etc. There is nothing wrong with reveling in this moment; it will stand in your memory for a long time as the point when your life took a turn for the better … all because you didn't give up!

Reversed: This card advises you not to throw out the baby with the bath water. It may on the surface appear as if you are not accomplishing all you hoped, but if you are willing to put forth some extra effort, you still have a chance to turn things around. Make your desire your number one priority (next to your own health, of course) and put all your energy towards those ends. Tell your friends and loved ones what is going on so they don't feel left out, then see about reaching for that brass ring. It is still within range if you build up your foundations.

Personal Notes

Wisteria

Gender: Male
Planet: Neptune
Element: Air
Magical Association:
Study, organization skills

Folklore/History

If you are planning to deliberate any matter, be it scholastic or spiritual, enjoy a cup of wisteria tea first. To improve your mental agility, dip the petals into batter and deep fry, then dust with sugar.

Interpretation

Upright: Wisteria tells that you will soon be welcoming a stranger to your home or life. The good feelings of the first meeting can lay the foundation for a future friendship, so put your best foot forward. This person could eventually become a life-mate, teacher, or lend important assistance to the question at hand.

   Reversed: You are warned to be leery of strangers bearing gifts. The odd salesman, unusual visit from a group you never heard of, or even a survey taker could well be a disguise or ruse. You do not have to crawl in your shell and hide, but keep your senses well tuned and a healthy portion of skepticism handy.

Personal Notes

Suggested Sources for Flowers

🌸 A wide variety of dried flowers are available at florists and craft and hobby shops, or you can make your own using various techniques of drying as described in Chapter Two.

🌸 Your own gardening efforts, greenhouses, and florists are the best sources for fresh flowers.

🌸 Photos and drawings of flowers can be found in Victorian garden books, children's books, coloring books, posters, home and garden magazines, or seed catalogs. In most of these instances, rather than spending a lot of money for something you will be cutting up, check with secondhand book or magazine distributors as well as thrift stores for reasonably priced copies.

CHAPTER FIVE

Herbs

*What is a weed? A plant whose virtues
have not been discovered.*

Ralph Waldo Emerson

While the use of herbs for cooking or health has its roots deep in antiquity, their long-reaching impressions on humanity are still being felt today. In recent years we have experienced the interest in natural medicine and use of non-chemical health aids growing rapidly alongside the study of companion gardening techniques.

In this manner we have begun preparing for our future, through the valuable information on alternative lifestyles left to us through history and our ancestors. "Folk medicine" and lore about herbs was central to living even at the turn of the century. These people had a deep abiding trust that superstition and magical associations could improve their life.

The language of flowers includes some plants which could prove very useful to your personal oracle ... and to your life as well!

Agrimony

Gender: Male
Planet: Jupiter
Element: Air
Magical Associations:
Protection, sleep

Folklore/History

Throughout the Middle Ages, this was one of the most popular blossoms to be applied to wounds as a poultice. Agrimony produces small five-petaled flowers in July and August which are high in tannin, and may be boiled in water and strained for an effective gargle, or applied to the skin to relieve insect bites and acne.

Magically, when in the home or garden, agrimony is believed to send negativity back to the instigator and to detect the presence of witches. A sprig under your pillow is believed to aid in peaceful sleep.

Interpretation

Upright: Agrimony indicates thankfulness and gratitude, yet it is some-how ambiguous whether this is given or received by the querent. Whatever position this card takes in a layout, it portends circumstances where appreciative attitudes are called for, and provided freely, with fullness of heart.

Reversed: Unrequited love, unappreciated effort, a thankless job, or energy which bears no fruit are at the heart of the situation. Be it directly relating to the querent or to someone near him or her, some real emotional support is needed here to handle these circumstances with grace and a stiff upper lip. This card reminds us to be thankful for the little things in life, especially those around us who give unselfishly of their time. Those that serve, likewise need service.

Personal Notes

Aloe

Gender: Feminine
Planet: Moon
Element: Water
Magical Associations:
Protection, luck, healing

Folklore/History

Considered a drugstore in a flowerpot, aloe is the number one home remedy for burns and poison ivy. Dioscorides, a Greek physician and herbalist, recorded the use of this plant as early as 2,000 years ago. It is believed that Alexander the Great conquered Madagascar to insure his army would be well supplied with the herb for their wounds. Cleopatra was said to massage aloe into her skin every day to preserve her beauty.

While aloe is usually not thought of in a flowering sense, it does bear large tubular buds of a yellow or orange-red coloration, and grows fairly well in a wide variety of climates. Transplanting it to an outdoor setting can be very tricky, however, so if you want some handy all year round, a house plant is probably best.

Keep aloe in your home to treat injuries due to household accidents, or place it in a wreath with garlic to insure health and prosperity. Aloe gel needs no oil or cream added to function perfectly well for anointing in rituals for health and safety.

Interpretation

Upright: Aloe's message in the Victorian language of flowers has to do with our superstitions and how we interpret signs in our life. If erect, the card indicates that certain events are soon to occur which need your attention. An odd coordination of unusual circumstances will prove very important for your spiritual or personal growth. The advice here is to stay attuned and aware. Do not just shrug these occurrences off as coincidence. The universe is trying to tell you something, so listen closely.

Reversed: The aloe may indicate a missed opportunity or a lack of perception, be it personal, spiritual, or in matters of love. Someone or something is presenting signals to you which need your attention, but for some reason you are too occupied with other matters to notice.

On another level, transposition of this card may also be a warning to you not to over-spiritualize the mundane. While folklore and superstition can be very powerful and useful, there are times when science and common sense must have their place. Not all things which happen in your life have to have deeper meaning. Remember to enjoy life for what it is … instead of searching so hard for what you think it should be that you miss the moment.

Personal Notes

Angelica

Gender: Male
Planet: Sun
Element: Fire
Magical Associations:
Protection, vision, healing

Folklore/History

This eight-foot tall herb is nothing other than stately when full grown. It is happiest near seas and mountain streams, and has been used throughout history as a ward against evil. If planted near the perimeter of a home it is thought to protect the occupants, and if the root is carried it is believed to insure good luck.

With its slightly licorice-like taste, it is quite edible in soups or salads or as a meat garnish. The stems and roots can be prepared much as asparagus with butter. In decoction form, angelica is a good aid to digestion and bronchial difficulties.

Interpretation

Upright: Angelica is the card of divine inspiration and muse. Be it writing, painting, music, or whatever most inspires you, there is abundant energy to help create something truly spectacular! Beyond this, the people around you are likewise being supportive which lends emotional buoyancy to your project. Don't be surprised if the results of anything you attempt right now are close to miraculous; you have the attention of the Great Spirit, and as long as you maintain proper perspective, you can do marvelous things which will have long-lasting effects.

Reversed: Obstacles and discouragement to your artistic endeavors seem to plague you. However, the blockage is not without cause. You may be trying to proceed too quickly or finish a project for the sake of just getting it done. However, there is more at stake here than just a deadline, so slow down and allow inspiration its own way. If you really follow inner guidance here, those waiting will do so with patient understanding.

Personal Notes

Balm

Gender: Feminine
Planet: Jupiter
Element: Water
Magical Associations:
Love, joy, improved mental
outlook, divination, prophesy

Folklore/History

Sometimes called lemon balm due to it bearing a scent very similar to the fruit, balm is an excellent component for love charms, especially if you bathe in it.

Medicinally it acts as a mild sedative, good in infusion form for fevers and to aid sleep. The herb is mentioned by Dioscorides for easing discomfort from insect bites, and doctors in ancient Arabia believed it improved the general spirits of their patients.

It may be utilized as any member of the mint family for flavor in cooking and salads, and when dried is a marvelous ingredient for any incense to which you would like to add the fresh, cleansing aroma of lemon.

Interpretation

Upright: A plant of sympathy, this card indicates that someone near you (perhaps even yourself) needs support, a good ear, and some positive input. This individual may be trying to be the proverbial island in the storm, but is quickly being swallowed by waves, even if he or she doesn't recognize it.

In this position, balm may also indicate a latent tendency toward the gift of a healer in your life, which up to now has been denied. Do not be afraid, and know that healing can take many forms from easing pain to helping bring sleep. It is rarely dramatic, and is a gentle art. This card is telling you that the opportunity exists to open the door of your spirit and let yourself become an instrument of divine energy.

Reversed: This card is a warning that you may be getting hardened in your attitudes towards others. An open hand and a warm heart are not signs of weakness, and are always welcome in the lives of others. Don't be afraid to help because propriety is constraining. Periodically toss "Miss Manners" aside and reach out. The results will not only change the person you helped, it will transform you!

For the healer, the inverted card warns that too much personal energy may have been extended in his or her art. Those that serve, likewise need service. An inherent problem with the gift of healing is the deep sense of responsibility and desire to help others which accompanies it. However, we cannot help anyone if we are overly tired, or if the well of self is empty. Do not ignore your own need for support, positive energy, and rest.

Personal Notes

Basil

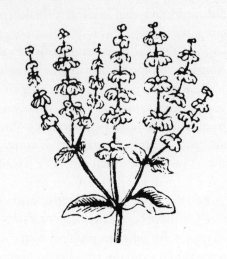

Gender: Male
Planet: Mars
Element: Fire
Magical Association:
Love, protection, sensitivity

Folklore/History

The scent of fresh basil is believed to promote sympathy between two people, so you may wish to use it as part of a peace offering to someone with whom you want to rebuild communications. Culpeper prescribed basil to women to help quicken labor, but warned not to smell it during pregnancy. For constipation or a headache, take one teaspoon of basil in a tea.

In some instances, basil is used to insure fidelity, create stronger feelings of love, and to aid the intuitive nature. It is also an excellent, long-lasting aromatic for magical sachets, charms, incense, or potpourri.

Interpretation

Upright: Basil indicates movement or haste. This card counsels you to move with all due swiftness on an opportunity being presented (or soon to come). If you do not seize the moment, relying on your instincts, you may be passed over. Like a specter, this opening is one which goes unnoticed by those around you, and therefore you might question its potential. Do not let others' lack of foresight dissuade you; listen to your inner voice.

In this capacity, basil may also be an indicator of change, especially in living situations. A new house or apartment, or even a move to another state could soon be on its way. This move is going to be a positive one for you, so stop fussing. The hardest part is making the first step. After that, just keep walking!

Reversed: Basil warns that you may have jumped too quickly into or out of a situation, specifically a relationship or job. The result of this movement is uncertain depending on what you do next, so the basil asks you to consider your subsequent steps carefully and seek that small voice within for insight. Do not allow your whims or the opinions of others to influence you right now. Proceed with caution.

Personal Notes

Broom

Gender: Male
Planet: Mars
Element: Air
Magical Associations:
Protection, purification, love
magic, divination, wind spells

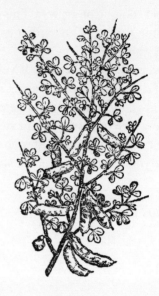

Folklore/History

Broom is an important herb to the magical community since it was probably first used as the name might imply, as a valued household implement. In many cultures, broom has been used for weddings (specifically jumping over a bundle to signify the new life), and over the years a formal broom has become the object of much superstition. Finding one in your new home, for example, is very good fortune, for you can then sweep the dust toward the center of the room and insure your luck is not cleaned away!

Broom flowers are quite edible and can be used in salad preparations, pickling, and wines. If you can get dried broom, you can also make your own magical decorations by binding it together and adding a few dried flowers appropriate to the season. It is a very appropriate herb to burn to cleanse a sacred space, or even use in place of an ordinary broom to scribe the circle.

Interpretation

Upright: Broom is the card of neatness and organization. You may feel as if the spring cleaning bug has bit you early, or the intense desire to reorder your home. Frequently this card appears because somehow your personal space has been disrupted either by circumstances or individuals, and the tidying is a means for you to reclaim your space. This card may also be a counsel to take extra care in purifications on a spiritual level. Your home is your sanctuary. Treat it accordingly.

Reversed: Everything seems scattered and messy, even things that you thought were in their place. There seems to be a lack of focus right now, a turmoil that is turning everything upside-down. Usually when this occurs it indicates a clearing away of old ways, outmoded habits, and all the emotional confusion that goes with breaking cycles. Frequently when our lives are disrupted it is a way for Spirit to get our attention. Listen to that voice, and stop fighting positive change. Just like a snake, we periodically have to shed our old skins in order to grow.

Personal Notes

Chamomile

Gender: Male
Planet: Sun
Element: Water
Magical Association:
Money, sleep, love, purification

Folklore/History

Throughout history, chamomile has been favored for bringing out blond highlights in hair, and it has long been employed as a soothing tea for children and adults alike. When cooled, chamomile tea may also be applied to the skin to act as an insect repellent. For a hair rinse, use four tablespoons of flowers to a pint of water boiled twenty minutes and strained. Interestingly enough, this rinse can also be sprinkled in your garden to discourage infestation.

Known to the Greeks as the apple of the earth, steamed chamomile leaves and flowers ease a toothache, are good in creams, and the plants themselves make a lovely addition to any magical garden.

To make a chamomile beer for rituals to restore peace, blend four ounces of chamomile flowers with one ounce of ginger root, one ounce of cream of tartar, two pounds of sugar, one and a half gallons of water, and just a hint of orange rind. Warm these over a low flame until the sugar is dissolved. Allow the mixture to cool, strain, and add half a package of active yeast. Let this liquid work on your stove or other secure area for one week before bottling with loose corks. After ten weeks, you may secure the lids tightly, and in another month you may drink it.

Interpretation

Upright: Chamomile is both energy and peacefulness. When brewed in a tea it helps us relax and revitalize ourselves, and such is the advice of this card. Take a little time to fortify the well of self. You may be overwhelmed by projects or responsibility, or simply have not given yourself enough personal time lately. Whatever the case, remember to pamper the temple of your soul too. If you don't, you may find yourself with a cold or other minor malady as a gentle nudge from the universe to sit down!

Chamomile may also indicate an increase in personal energy for a specific purpose, frequently a creative one. You may find you are dreaming or doodling constantly. If this is the case, take a closer look and keep notes! You are being given a project or idea which later may manifest itself into a wonderful opportunity.

Reversed: Chamomile asks you to check the direction of your personal energy. The feeling here is that it is scattered and bouncing merrily around without focus. You may feel as if you cannot think clearly, or find that you are frustrated with an inability to cope with the juggling act going on in your life. If so, stop for a while. Delegate some responsibility to other people and let yourself breathe. You need to center your energy and reclaim the reigns of your life before trying to ride off on another quest.

Personal Notes

Fennel

Gender: Masculine
Planet: Mercury
Element: Fire
Magical Association:
Protection, purification, healing

Folklore/History

Historically this herb was often used in rites to honor Dionysus. The Greek name for fennel is *marathon*, meaning to grow thin, because it was long believed to aid as an appetite suppressant. In magic, fennel has often been placed in a doorway on Midsummer's eve to turn away any negative energy.

The small yellow flowers of this herb have a taste similar to anise and are a good addition to salads or to season fish. Steep a bit in rum or water for an effective mouthwash and breath freshener, or make it into a tea to soothe the stomach, especially colic in babies. The blossoms when mixed with cream of tartar will produce a yellow to brown dye for wool.

Interpretation

Upright: An herb of protection, this card in your spread indicates the need to gather your strength. Take extra precautions regarding your health and well-being. Rest, and prepare for the storm which lingers just over the horizon. In this instance the rains will be swift but heavy, and you will need a good sense of humor to help keep yourself afloat.

Reversed: The fennel emphasizes personal weaknesses which need to be worked on. Possibly bad habits, old fears, and other little faults begin to nag at you, demanding some attention to cope with them in a positive, transformational manner. Don't be discouraged by what you see, however. Knowing our weaknesses and being able to face them honestly builds character and a solid foundation from which we can learn to love ourselves.

Personal Notes

Mint

Gender: Male
Planet: Mercury
Element: Air
Magical Associations:
Protection, healing, travel
spells, love

Folklore/History

Mint boasts a long line of associations from Hecate to the Pharisees who paid their tithes with mint. Pliny felt it was the most lovely of all herbs, and the Greeks were known to use mint widely in their temple rites.

Various types of mint, most specifically pennyroyal, have been used for thousands of years to combat insects, and fresh leaves from this plant were often strewn in the medieval home to help combat odors.

Mint tea is an effective aid to cramps and stomachache. If your hands are chapped, try making a mint water from half a gallon of liquid to one cup of herb brought to a boil. This may be placed in an airtight container and used as needed.

To make a refreshing bath tincture which improves circulation, take equal quantities of mint, bay, thyme, rosemary, marjoram, lavender, and lemon balm and let them steep in hot water. Repeat until the water has a very strong scent from the herbs. To this add a cup of brandy to act as a preservative. Bottle and pour into your bath water as desired.

Interpretation

Upright: This card is an indication that now is an excellent time to begin developing various qualities to improve your self-worth. What you might have thought of in the past as impossible to change, you presently have the energy and inner strength to pursue, but try and focus on one important item at a time. If you scatter your energy too much, this opportunity may be lost.

    Reversed: A suggestion to look to your personal motivations for the question at hand (or those of other individuals). Somewhere along the way you will discover that appearances have been deceptive. Perhaps a job was misrepresented to you, or the reasons for a particular favor. Whatever the case, this card warns to move forward cautiously, considering not only your own conscience but the possibility that you may be going in the wrong direction altogether, having been lead astray. In either scenario, this is the opportunity to straighten things out so you can make your decisions confidently.

Personal Notes

Mistletoe

Gender: Male
Planet: Sun
Element: Air
Magical Association:
Fertility, health, searching,
romance, legal matters (carried)

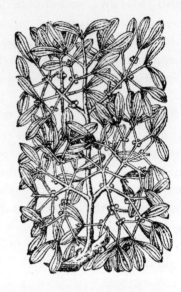

Folklore/History

Mistletoe was sacred to the peoples of ancient Europe as a symbol of immortality. It has long been associated with both medicine and magic. The Druids called it "the plant that heals all ills." They so prized the mistletoe that it was only gathered in ritual manner using a golden sickle. The Teutons believed that warriors who carried a sprig would be invincible.

This plant flowers in mid-spring and early summer. Medicinally, the leaves are sometimes infused into water to help reduce high blood pressure and ease migraines.

Interpretation

Upright: Mistletoe upright in a spread is an indication that certain technical difficulties you have recently experienced will soon be resolved. A major appliance or your car may have broken down, but somehow the means will come your way so that everything works out in your favor.

Because of its long association with romance, mistletoe may also indicate for the single person a new "significant other" who is terribly passionate and sensitive in nature. For married couples, this signifies a reawakening of feelings which may have gotten lost along the way. A new intuitive connection can be formed now to help stabilize the relationship.

Reversed: The mistletoe portends all manner of technologically based frustrations. It may seem as if everything around you is falling apart at the same time. Frequently these types of problems will occur in sets of three over a period of three days, weeks, or months.

In regard to relationships, the overturned mistletoe is not a good sign. Romantic feelings seem to be lost, and an almost disinterested attitude has replaced them. It may be that a third party has entered the picture and disrupted things, a disagreement has disturbed communications, or that the season for your association is past. This mistletoe cautions you not to move too quickly or make rash decisions based on emotions instead of serious thought. This may only be a temporary cooling instead of winter. You might give up something very valuable if you don't wait to see what the next wind brings before making final judgment.

Personal Notes

Moss

Gender: Feminine
Planet: Saturn
Element: Earth
Magical Association:
Luck, love, poppet magic

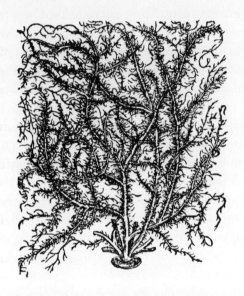

Folklore/History

The simple ground moss is so unassuming that except to regard it briefly on a trip through the woods it might otherwise go unnoticed by many. Its usefulness to the creative magician, however, should not be underestimated. Many practitioners recommend using dried moss and appropriate herbs to stuff poppets, especially those created for fire festivals.

Two other applications were popular during the Victorian era. One was binding bits of moss to a picture frame which contained pressed flowers. This way the entire art work reflected the natural element. Another method consisted of applying dried mosses to a hoop of straw with fine wire as the basis for a herb wreath. To this foundation, any number of dried herbs and flowers could be added for lovely, thematic, and functional results.

Interpretation

Upright: The plant of maternal love, the moss may indicate that a young person, or someone young of heart, has come into your life who really needs guidance and support. This individual is impulsive, naive, and very unworldly to the point where he or she is easily taken advantage of or manipulated. There is vast potential here for a magical student-teacher relationship to grow if fostered in the correct, trusting atmosphere. Likewise, an abiding friendship may develop if you are patient and remember not to assume any knowledge on the other's part. Like a child who must learn to walk, much of what you will share with him or her is new, even on the most mundane and practical levels. Dig deep into your well of experience and share as much wisdom as you can. Both your life and his or hers will be enriched for the effort.

Reversed: The moss can suggest several things. It may be a warning to you against being too much of the "mother hen." All parents (literally or figuratively) must eventually let their children walk on their own, trusting in what they have taught them. In this scenario, you must cut the apron strings between you and the person involved, and hope for the best.

On another level it may indicate that you are the one who is being naive, capricious, or "youthful" in your outlook regarding a specific situation. For some reason you have gotten caught up in the wave of the moment and lost perspective. The moss warns you to step back for a moment and take a critical look at your present actions. Consider if it were someone else, what advice you would give him or her, and take that advice. If a trusted friend has been trying to get a message through to you, now is the time to listen.

Personal Notes

Motherwort

Gender: Feminine
Planet: Venus
Element: Fire
Magical Association:
Improving moods, vitality,
wishes

Folklore/History

On the ninth day of the ninth month, the Japanese celebrate this herb which symbolizes life itself. It is perhaps because of this belief that motherwort is included as one of the ingredients in saki. On this day, a special cup of saki decorated with the herb is passed hand to hand as a wish to friends for long, prosperous living.

To make a conserve (appropriate as a gift to friends and loved ones), slowly mix one pound of crushed flowers with two pounds of sugar. Store this in an airtight container and apply it to toast and scones as desired. The longer it ages, the better it becomes!

Interpretation

Upright: In the language of flowers, this blossom indicates hidden love, but for your oracle it does not have to be just love of an individual. Concealed passion can have to do with dreams, goals, and desires too. For example, perhaps you have a "crazy idea" but are afraid to share it because of other people's expected responses. The advice of this card upright is to let your ideas or feelings cook for a while longer. They have great potential, but you are too close to have real perspective at this point. Time and careful deliberation will grant the greatest rewards.

Reversed: This card is telling you to go ahead and bring to light the hidden matter. While you may still feel a little uncertain about it, you will meet with a favorable or surprising response. The enthusiasm may not take the form that you hoped, but it will prove helpful and somehow settle the questions nagging your heart.

Personal Notes

Nightshade

Gender: Feminine
Planet: Saturn
Element: Fire
Magical Association:
Structure, manifestation,
increasing power, hidden
matters, cleansing magical tools

Folklore/History

The deadly nightshade is one of the most lethal poisons known to man. (It was one of the herbs used to bring death to Shakespeare's Juliet.) Because of this, it must be used by the magical practitioner with great caution and appropriate care. If you do choose to use it as a spell component or add a bit to water to consecrate your tools, please make sure you keep it well out of the reach of children or pets.

Interpretation

Upright: The deadly nightshade is the card of secrets, the unknown, the void, and death. Upright, it tends to indicate drastic, instinctive change which leaves you depending on an uncertain factor. You may feel lead to move to another state without the assurance of a job, for example. It may also signify breaking free of a cycle, negative relationship, or habit in the process.

This is a powerful card indicating that forces beyond your control are at work in your life. Much will remain hidden to you, like shadows which you can't quite catch sight of, until your step of faith has come to a conclusion. There will be some honest fears and ambivalence to grapple with, from those around you and even in your own heart, but don't give up on the vision you have glimpsed! It can become a reality.

Reversed: This card portends a change or death of a more painful nature. It can be a literal death, or simply that of an outmoded form of thinking, but whatever it is, the transformation will not be an easy one.

Nightshade speaks to us of poisons in our life … perhaps an addiction, bitterness, anger, and other forms of human failings which can prove emotionally or physically damaging. If this is the case, realize that you are the one who must take the first step towards wholeness. While you may feel alone, abandoned, and without any guideposts to lead your way, it is for good reason. Fate is asking you to develop a willingness to help yourself. Until you really want to care about the quality of your life, no one else can aid you.

Personal Notes

Parsley

Gender: Male
Planet: Mercury
Element: Air
Magical Associations:
Protection, purification, desire

Folklore/History

A natural breath freshener, Romans often chewed a bit of parsley to cover the aroma of wine on their tongues after a festival and to aid digestion. Associated with Persephone, parsley was also once believed to be a garland for Hercules.

Parsley grows readily in temperate zones, and in tincture form it offers high quantities of vitamins A and C along with other healthful minerals. So healthful, in fact, it was frequently fed to race horses to improve their stamina. It is a valued culinary herb in France, used readily for sauté and poultry. In Japan it is deep fried as a tempura dish. It can also be added to your bath to help cleanse the skin.

Interpretation

Upright: Entertainment and feasting are on their way! This card indicates a pleasant period of socialization, visiting with friends, parties, and a few unexpected surprises. In many instances it is a well-deserved break from daily labors, and is perhaps even long overdue. No matter how tempted you are to jump back on the productivity bandwagon, try to simply relax and enjoy yourself, realizing that this activity is important for your well-being right now.

Reversed: A sense of retreat, desire to quietly hide in the shadows, and foreboding are indicated by parsley reversed. You have removed yourself purposefully from an important group in your life, either due to embarrassment or miscommunications. If possible, try to rectify this situation. Re-examine what happened with discernment and see if there is a way to rebuild this bridge. It is not one which should be burned behind you. However, if other people are unwilling to forgive or forget, the attempt to heal the wound will give you personal peace of mind which will be important in days ahead.

The parsley can also be speaking to you about personal eating habits, specifically overindulgence when you are upset or nervous. The advice here is to learn about your own routines so that negative ones can be broken.

Personal Notes

Rosemary

Gender: Male
Planet: Sun
Element: Fire
Magical Association:
Mental agility, sleep,
purification, healing

Folklore/History

A traditional ingredient in Hungarian beauty techniques since the fourteenth century, and popular in incense during the sixteenth, this herb was known and used in many other lands, long before. The Romans considered it a sacred herb which brought joy to the living and peace to the dead. Legend has it that if a rosemary bush grows in your garden, it means the woman is the head of your house. Rosemary was frequently added to bridal bouquets because of it symbolism of love and remembrance.

Rosemary is prescribed in tea form to ease the effects of the flu or mental strain. In wine it acts as a digestive aid, and in tincture form (one pint of water, one ounce of sage, one ounce of rosemary) it is an excellent hair rinse for brunettes. Rosemary buds make a good facial steam to perk up the skin.

You may also prepare a wonderful cough syrup with this herb by combining one cup of warm honey, a slice each of orange, lemon, and ginger, a whole clove of garlic, and two teaspoons of rosemary. Keep this in an airtight container, and then strain the mixture when the garlic looks almost transparent. The added advantage to this recipe is that it makes a wonderful glaze for chicken and ham.

Interpretation

Upright: This is very definitely a social card. Here, your time spent with other people seems to revitalize your energy and give you some really wonderful memories for days ahead. The rosemary may portend a marriage for yourself or a dear friend. Other celebratory occasions are also indicated, and you should make every attempt to attend them. If you don't, you will be missing a very special opportunity for fellowship and fun long remembered.

Reversed: The rosemary can be speaking to you in several different ways. The first might be a tendency to be too outgoing to the point where your personal energy has dwindled. You may be burning the candle on both ends and quickly running out of wax. Similarly the rosemary may warn that other people are taking advantage of your good nature and drawing from your seemingly endless well of strength. Don't feel you have to say "yes" all the time just to make other people happy. Your first obligation is to your own well-being.

Alternatively, the rosemary may portend an awkward social situation. A mishap at a party, harsh words spoken in front of company, or other embarrassing circumstances might come up to taint the festivities. If this is the case, do your best to smooth things out so everyone is put at ease. Just because you stick your foot in your mouth, doesn't mean you can't pull it out!

Personal Notes

Saffron

Gender: Male
Planet: Sun
Element: Air
Magical Association:
Uplifting moods, psychic
energy, joy, healing, moving
the winds (Persia)

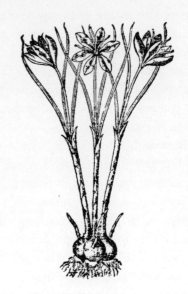

Folklore/History

This member of the crocus family has been a part of human heritage for a very long time. It is valued because it takes nearly 35,000 flowers to make one ounce of spice. It is also used to prepare one of the most beautiful yellow dyes available. The Greeks took advantage of this, making it a royal hue, and adorning their gods and heroes in robes of saffron. King Solomon's garden had a whole plot of this herb, and during the fourteenth through eighteenth centuries was one of the most popular medicinal herbs in Europe.

For health reasons, saffron is rarely used any more due to its toxicity in doses of one-third ounce or more. Even so, it has remained a favored spice for bouillabaisse, cakes, bread, cookies, lamb, and fish.

A tasty pudding can be made by infusing a cup of warm milk with several sprigs of saffron and adding this to two ounces of butter rubbed in flour, one ounce of blanched almonds, a dash of cinnamon, and two ounces of sugar. Warm this over a low flame and serve when thickened.

Interpretation

Upright: Mirth and laughter are the gift of this spice. Circumstances in your life are far less heavy right now. Burdens are few, bills are paid, work is going smoothly, and generally everything seems right with the world. You find an improvement in your sense of humor and ability to laugh at the odd twists in life.

This is a period of pure enjoyment where you can take a long, deep breath and feel no pressure or worries. With this in mind, saffron might also portend a brief vacation.

Reversed: A sense of foreboding, melancholy, or general gloom seems to hang over your head like a cloud. The only problem is that you have no idea why; or if you do, it's something you have no control over. When times like this come, reach out to your friends and family for a little extra support. Cry it out and allow your tears to cleanse you. Call on the winds to come and move the clouds away from you so that a smile can return in place of the frown.

Personal Notes

Sage

Gender: Male
Planet: Jupiter
Element: Air
Magical Association:
Insight, fertility, longevity,
wishes

Folklore/History

Derived from the Latin word *salvare* which means "to cure" or "salvation," the Romans gathered sage with great ritualistic care. They used no iron tools, wore white tunics, and had well-washed feet. Considered a cure-all during the Middle Ages, sage was the obligatory ingredient in almost all foods and medicines. So much was the case that for a very long time three crops of sage a year had to be planted and harvested in Yugoslavia to meet the demand.

Today, sage still has many applications. It is a good insect repellent as most strong aromatics, is proving beneficial to people with high blood sugar, acts as a digestive aid, and in the form of an infusion will even help irregular menstruation.

To make a flavorful sage tea, use one ounce of the herb to a pint of boiling water. Add a bit of orange and lemon. This mixture is also an effective gargle and breath freshener.

Interpretation

Upright: Much to your surprise you have caught the cleaning bug! You suddenly have a strong desire to clean, sort, fold, scrub, and set your domicile into refreshed order. This new thrust towards domestic virtues is kind of like a nesting instinct to help mark your territory and really make your house feel like a home. Go with the energy. Pay particular attention to making your house most accessible and comfortable for the people and animals which reside there. Remember, this is your castle ... even if it is one room on the tenth floor!

This yearning can also manifest itself in another way, that of doting over people like a mother hen. You may find yourself fussing excessively and fidgeting around your friends and family, but the attention is enjoyed. You have changed your focus to your home-unit, and that's always important.

Reversed: Chaotic, disorderly, and unkempt are the words that come quickly to mind. You have avoided your chores at home to the point where there isn't a clean dish left. Dirty clothes are piled knee deep, and dust bunnies threaten to take over. Other members of your household may be quickly losing their patience with you, causing a great deal of tension and animosity.

The advice of this card is clean up your act. Be more considerate and gentle in your demeanor and stop making excuses for being lazy. Even if you live alone, you owe yourself a certain amount of clean, ordered living space just from a health standpoint. The way you treat your living space is often quite indicative of how you really think of yourself. What thoughts does your home reflect?

Personal Notes

Thistle

Gender: Male
Planet: Mars
Element: Fire
Magical Association:
Strength, courage, protection

Folklore/History

A long-standing symbol of Scotland, the thistle is sometimes known colo-quially as the cardoon. In magic, the thistle is especially effective in any rituals for pets. In the kitchen, it may be prepared and served much like asparagus or Brussels sprouts. Thistles have also been known to be used to prepare a rather biting punch consisting of whiskey, vermouth, tarragon, clove, and several boiled flower heads. Should you try this mixture, it would be best served for fire-related festivals.

Interpretation

Upright: A sense of defiant independence and the physical endurance to follow through on your intentions exist right now. For some reason you have been pressed against the wall and reacted with bold rebellion. This matter is not just one person's doing. Everyone involved has handled the situation badly, basing action on their hearts instead of their heads. So, don't blame the "other guy" without pointing a few fingers at yourself too. You have a choice to make, but can do so with dignity instead of dissension.

Reversed: The thistle is speaking to you about your sense of self. Too frequently you are willing to go with the majority rule, even if it directly conflicts with personal morals. This herb asks to you listen to your inner voice, and take courage as a friend. Don't be afraid to stand up for yourself and causes you think are just. Heed the counsel of those wiser than you, but do so measuring their words against your own standards. Try to discover who you really are, what you believe, and grow towards that goal.

Personal Notes

Thyme

Gender: Feminine
Planet: Venus
Element: Water
Magical Association:
Courage, energy

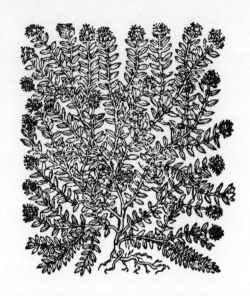

Folklore/History

Born from the tears of gentle Helena, thyme grows wild in the Mediterranean. The Egyptians and Etruscans incorporated this herb into their embalming techniques, the Greeks burned thyme to honor their gods, and Romans used thyme in water to enhance beauty.

The written word has traveled far and wide about the attributes of thyme. Aristotle felt that honey made from this herb was so delectable that it was really cultivated from stars and rainbows. Early herbalists recommended it to relieve pain in joints, stimulate circulation, and as an appetite aid. These uses are still employed today, plus that of easing a cough and improving physical energy. The dried flowers of thyme will even help keep moths away from linen!

Persians enjoyed snacking on these flowers, and their culinary use is well-known, favored for soup, stuffings, and seasoning lamb, beef, and pork. To make a vinegar excellent for salads or to marinate meat, take your favorite vinegar (three cups) and add several pieces of fresh garlic, two tablespoons of oregano, basil, and thyme and warm over a low flame. This can be safely stored and used up to a year.

Interpretation

Upright: Courage and energy in the face of adversity is the message of the thyme. No matter your question, if you look deep within yourself you will find a wellspring of fortitude waiting to see you through. This is a learning experience, and one which calls on you to hold your own even when the rug has been pulled away. If you can retain your determination, you will find the rewards are well worth the temporary frustrations.

Reversed: Timidity and hesitation, the inability to make a firm decision. You have been wavering on the fence for too long, and if you don't determine to settle things soon, the moment will be lost altogether. The test in this matter is not finding the perfect solution, but just resolving to act instead of sitting on the sidelines watching life go by.

Personal Notes

Witch Hazel

Gender: Male
Planet: Sun
Element: Fire
Magical Associations:
Cleansing, healing, beauty

Folklore/History

Native to most moist regions of North America, literally millions of gallons of witch hazel tincture are sold every year as a health and beauty aid. In this form, it does have mild astringent qualities, and as a tea is excellent for mouth and throat infections.

In India, witch hazel leaves are used in compress form for sore eyes and headaches. They will also grant relief from insect bites and mild strains. In some areas of the world, the limber branches have been used to make archery bows.

If you are having skin irritations, try tossing a handful of witch hazel in your bath water to help bring soothing relief.

Interpretation

Upright: The witch hazel upright in your spread indicates you are totally enchanted with a person or an idea, to the point where your good judgment may be failing. The counsel of this card is to enjoy what you have, but not to immerse yourself totally, thus allowing other equally important matters to go by the wayside. In relationships, this card usually portends "puppy love" that quickly burns itself out if not nurtured properly. In most situations it is a sign of premature enthusiasm which can set you up for a severe disappointment. No matter how zealous you may feel, try and keep one foot on the ground.

Reversed: Not good news, by any means. Something you have hoped for or a relationship you desired has not come to fruition. There is a sense of disillusionment and frustration in this card, and unfortunately in most cases the fault lies in your own lap. Pressing too hard or trying to make your influence felt in inappropriate ways is usually the culprit here, but despite the sadness, it is a situation from which you can learn valuable lessons, especially pertaining to your interpersonal communications. You will need to take some time to recoup and heal the wounds, but while you do, don't overlook the opportunity for positive introspection.

Personal Notes

Yarrow

Gender: Female
Planet: Venus
Element: Water
Magical Association:
Courage, mental strength, love

Folklore/History

Once believed to have been used by Achilles to heal, yarrow is respected in the Orient because of its association with the I Ching (see Introduction). Sacred to the horned god, this flower is often used in handfastings.

History suggests that it has been used by mankind for almost 60,000 years. In the seventeenth century, a witch was tried for employing it in a love incantation. More recently, the Shakers have recommended its use for hemorrhage and coughs.

Yarrow does have a mild anti-inflammatory ability if applied as a poultice. It is also a good astringent if added to skin lotions.

Interpretation

Upright: Conflicting emotions, confusing choices, and diverse opinions are at the heart of your question. There are too many cooks, too many experts, and all these voices leave your head swimming. Your best friend right now would be some privacy, away from all the speculation, where you can really think.

The advice of this card is to do just that. Retreat for a while, think things through. Take into account the ideas which have been expressed, but don't let them overwhelm your ability to judge matters for yourself.

Reversed: An end to bewilderment and turmoil. You have either reached a definite decision or something has happened to clear up all the chaos of the last few weeks. The final outcome is not known to be favorable or unfavorable, simply settled, which in itself brings a sense of relief.

Personal Notes

Suggested Uses for Herbs

In previous chapters, I have already touched briefly on how herbs have historically been used in divination. Besides this, there are many ways of employing herbs above and beyond the creation of your divinatory tool. Consider the following examples.

- ❧ Use various herbs as discussed in the first part of Chapter Three in a pendulum for divining "yes" or "no" type questions. Remember to use an herb which is somehow affiliated with the central theme of your question.

- ❧ Purchase the herbal Tarot presently available through U.S. Toys and Games and see if that meets your needs or inspires ideas on making your own.

- ❧ Get any books by Scott Cunningham, Jude Williams, or Louise Riotte on herbalism, or refer to the bibliography herein for other texts which could be used to research the symbolism for your oracle, incenses, herbal potions, anointing oils, decorations for your sacred space, etc. *Please take special care to insure that any herbal preparation you make for use on the skin or as a magical "elixir" is safe by modern standards.* This is best accomplished by comparing three unrelated sources on herbal arts for common usage and conferring with people you know to be proficient with herbal skills.

Suggested Sources for Herbs

- ❧ Check your yellow pages for organic herb suppliers. Many health food shops or international supermarkets carry a wide range of herbs, even in bulk. More than likely your local cooperative will be able to give you a few names of herb growers or suppliers in your area.

❧ For photos and drawings of herbs, visit your grocery store (the bottles which many herbs come in have good pictures). You can also watch for these at garage sales. Other excellent sources are seed catalogs, garden shops, old encyclopedias, field guides to herbs, and herb-based magazines.

CHAPTER SIX

Trees and Shrubs

A fool sees not the same tree that a wise man sees.

William Blake

When we look at a tree, we think immediately of foundations, roots, and grounding. The long life of these beautiful plants is a standing reminder to us of strength, perseverance, and durability. Besides the symbolic element, it is nice to have a gift from nature as part of your divinatory tools. I do recommend, however, that you do not "harvest" wood from trees, but watch for fallen branches instead. Tearing a limb from its home often leaves an opening for insect infestation.

The wood from a specific tree may be chosen as the base for your oracle according to personal preference (see Chapter Two). You can also use a picture of the tree or a dried, pressed leaf or blossom as part of your divination system's symbols.

Almond

Gender: Male
Planet: Mercury
Element: Air
Magical Association:
Money, healing, protection

Folklore/History

Believed to prevent drunkenness if eaten, or to guard against the evil eye, there was a time when someone might have climbed a flowering almond tree to ensure the success of a business deal. Magical wands are still often made from an almond branch, as almond is aligned with the element of air, and if you keep an almond nut in your pocket you can expect to find a surprise!

To make a cream which is excellent for the skin and magically identified with healing and prosperity, blend together half a cup of almond oil, four inches of an eight-inch white taper candle, two teaspoons of rose water, and one almond flower (if available). Warm this mixture until the wax is completely melted and remove the flower. Beat until the liquid takes on a cold-cream texture, then store in an airtight container. Use as desired.

Interpretation

Upright: Almond is the tree of hope, watchfulness, and haste. If you have drawn this card upright it is a sign that better times are on their way.

However, there is a caution here about seeing or interpreting things which may not exist.

As you begin to see the first light after the clouds, wait a moment to be sure the rains have gone before making any decision. Watch for your boat to come in, but don't jump quickly onto each deck available until you are certain the vessel is secure and right for you. The full bloom of this card may also indicate having to choose from multiple, equally tempting opportunities, but do so with care.

Reversed: This card speaks of a dark period in life when you feel hope has left you. You may be unable to see anything positive about your situation; almost as if all is at a complete standstill. Try not to despair, however. All rich soil must periodically go fallow in order to reap even greater harvests the next season. This drought is only temporary, most likely not to last longer than four months or a turn of the Wheel. Be patient and constructively use this time to deal with the shadows inside yourself.

Personal Notes

Apple

Gender: Feminine
Planet: Venus
Element: Water
Magical Association:
Health, love, knowledge,
gardening

Folklore/History

Among the deities associated with the apple are Diana, Zeus, and Athena. Norse gods consumed the fruit of this tree daily to improve their vigor and youth. Thus the saying of "an apple a day" for health still exists. The apple is closely associated with self knowledge for boon or bane, and it is also a traditional fruit to employ in love divinations by twisting the stem.

Because the apple is a harvest fruit, apple pie is an appropriate treat for Samhain or any fall festival. Apple wood wands are excellent tools for rituals involving health or blessing your land, and apple blossoms on an altar for handfastings are tremendously beautiful.

Interpretation

Upright: The apple tree itself is the symbol of temptation, while its flowers are symbols of choice and desire. Combined in the upright position, this card is therefore regarded as a sign that you have some difficult decisions to make, frequently of a moral nature. The advice here is to consider all your options carefully before making a judgement you may regret for a long time. This is not a snap decision, and you should not allow the opinions of others to influence your final action as the consequences are very personal in nature.

Reversed: The apple indicates that you have given into your desires and may now feel remorse over that decision. Since your choice has already been made, it is best not to wallow in second-guesses. Instead, use this as an opportunity to discover the value of foresight and planning, then get on with the business of handling any repercussions in a positive manner. Personal responsibility is not always an easy lesson, but it is a very valuable one.

Personal Notes

Ash

Gender: Male
Planet: Sun
Element: Fire or Water
Magical Association:
Protection, prosperity, healing

Folklore/History

Ash is one of the trees Teutons thought may have been the Yggdrasil whose roots form the Earth and whose branches radiate into the stars. Odin had a spear of ash, and in many lands, ash is used as a charm against drowning. Poseidon, Thor, and Mars are also associated with the ash.

Ash wands or staffs are considered excellent tools for healing magic because of this tree's strong association with the characteristics of the water element. In matters of health, this element is emphasized.

Burn ash wood as part of any incense for financial stability or to honor Odin.

Interpretation

Upright: Some type of grandeur has entered your life, and you are now looked at by others in a new light. Time and honest efforts have proven your worth not only to yourself but to those around you. Frequently this is a business-related card which may portend a promotion or improved responsibilities. On a personal level, it may indicate the end of a long period of sickness or exhaustion which gives you a fresh lease on life. Either way, this is an exciting new beginning which is most merited.

Reversed: A gentle warning about not putting on airs or letting people put you on a pedestal. Remember the higher up you are the farther you have to fall, and the more painful those descents will be. While you have earned respect, it is always good to remember that you put your pants on the same as everyone else. In other words, don't get so far from your roots that you forget about the little, special things that make life worth savoring. If you are not careful here you could end up very lonely.

Personal Notes

Aspen

Gender: Masculine
Planet: Mercury
Element: Air
Magical Associations:
Language, protection from
theft, divination, prophesy

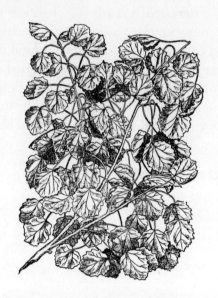

Folklore/History

Used by Native Americans to aid the symptoms of cold, flu, and allergies, the dried flowers of the aspen work well as components in incense, especially that which is being prepared to aid your ability to communicate clearly and definitively. Should you choose to prepare such a blend, you may wish to call on the goddess Inanna who governs oracular functions to aid your work.

Other uses for the aspen include placing a piece under your tongue to insure convincing speech. In many areas of the United States, an aspen branch is still used as a divining rod.

Interpretation

Upright: The tree of sensibility desires to sprout in your life. If you have drawn this card it indicates a need to slow down and use wisdom in your decision making. Do not overextend your money or personal energy right now, but use it prudently. Economy, frugality, and common sense are called for, not a tendency to jump in the pool without checking for water.

It may well be that a past mistake is haunting you, and drawing you back into an old, outmoded cycle. Now is the opportunity to break the chain and find new balance.

Reversed: This card indicates a pressing fear and a tendency towards extravagance. You may be trying to use energy or money as a means of making yourself feel welcome in a new group or situation. Lack of self-assurance is definitely a factor. Review your actions carefully and get to the root of them. Are you speaking loudly, joking too much, spending money you don't have, wearing unusual clothing? Things are not what makes you *you*. It's time to be honest and find out what's really bothering you, then deal with it head on.

Personal Notes

Birch

Gender: Female
Planet: Venus
Element: Water
Magical Association:
Protection, purification,
connection with nature

Folklore/History

A lovely complement to any rock garden, the birch is the queen of the forest and sacred to the god Thor. Her flowers come in the form of hanging catkins, with buds but no real petals, and the wood of the birch is often fashioned for a traditional witch's broom handle. The bark and leaves of this tree are also a mild analgesic and may be used in tincture form as an excellent mouth wash.

To make a refreshing drink for ritual, gather one quart of birch twigs in the spring and bring them to boil with one and a half gallons of water. To this add one quart of honey or sugar and stir over the flame until dissolved. Sugar will ferment much more quickly than honey, and produce a slightly different flavor, so choose this according to your taste and time constraints.

Once well-blended, allow the whole mixture to become lukewarm, then add half a package of active yeast, suspended in warm water, to the beer. This should be covered with a cloth and left on your stove for two weeks to work. Strain and bottle with corks loosely for another two weeks. You will be able to drink the beer at this time, but it gets better after about three months.

Interpretation

Upright: The birch is the lady of the woods in all her loveliness. In the upright position it indicates the genteel arts of grace, beauty, and charm being acquired in your life. You may notice an increase in your desire to care for other people. Now is also an excellent time to consider entertaining. The birch is a sign of a social period, a time of extroversion developing. New acquaintances who may become friends will start to bloom, and with them new attributes within you will likewise blossom.

    Reversed: This card indicates a rather negative attitude developing within. You may be testy, rude to those around you, overly sensitive, or just feeling anti-social. If this is the case, you need to find out the reasons behind your feelings and grapple with them soon. If you have had a problem with someone or a specific situation, air it out so that the winds of change can revitalize a more productive mood.

    Inverted this card can also warn that you are getting out of touch with the natural world. Too much metal, cement, and busyness have surrounded you, when what you need right now is some fresh air and trees to ground yourself once more. The counsel here is to find some time, even a few hours, to go to the country and reconnect yourself with the spirit of the land. You will find your mood much improved for the effort.

Personal Notes

Chestnut

Gender: Male
Planet: Jupiter
Element: Fire (the nut, Air)
Magical Association:
Love and awareness

Folklore/History

In Europe, chestnuts were sometimes left as an offering to ancestors on Samhain or Halloween. A traditional holiday roasting nut which represents the hope of spring. In the early history of the United States, chestnut wood was often used for telephone and telegraph poles as well as railroad ties. The nuts in powdered form may be used as an effective starch substitute.

Interpretation

Upright: The chestnut tree in bloom signifies some pleasant extravagance soon to manifest in your life. Just like a bit of starlight gathering at your feet, someone might give you a decadent gift for no reason, you may win a raffle, find a twenty-dollar bill on the sidewalk, or some other good fortune will come your way just when you needed it most.

    Reversed: This card warns not to give too much time and attention to "things." Despite the world's views, he or she who has the most toys does not always win, at least not spiritually. It may be that you have been focusing too much of your time and energy on moneymaking schemes or work while neglecting other items such as your family, meditation, proper rest, etc. The chestnut advises to remind yourself of what is truly valuable and lasting: love.

Personal Notes

Elder

Gender: Female
Planet: Venus
Element: Water
Magical Association:
Protection, symbolic magic
(especially for healing), sleep

Folklore/History

Judas is believed to have hanged himself from an elder. The white flowers of this tree are sacred to the Goddess, thus they are excellent additions to ritual baths, for blessings, and to protect the home. In France, apples are packed in elder flowers in the belief that they will enhance the flavor and longevity of the fruit. Interestingly enough, elder flower water is also a good treatment for sunburns, and the leaves of the elder are often made into ointments for bruises and itching.

To make a cleansing vinegar for the skin, take one part flowers steeped in twelve parts warm vinegar and soak for two weeks. Strain and use as desired. For a traditional elder flower water, use two quarts spring water and two quarts elder petals and bring them to a boil over low flame. To this add one and a half quarts of rum or spirits, then cool and strain. Besides its other uses, this liquid can also be applied to toothaches.

To prepare an elder flower cream, excellent for softening the skin, take two ounces of almond oil, half an ounce of wax, one ounce of lanolin or cocoa butter, and three ounces of elder flower water, warming them all together until well incorporated. Beat lightly while cooling until it takes on a creamy consistency. Store in an airtight container and use as needed.

Interpretation

Upright: Release elder to the winds with the whisper of a name, and that person will be blessed. In this case, the blessing comes to you. The elder in bloom is an indication of newly grown empathic abilities within yourself. You may soon discover that you have a better understanding of others' situations, more clearly defined relationships, and better communication skills. Continue to hone these new gifts as they exhibit themselves.

Wherever this card appears upright in a spread, it may also indicate some type of charity drive which you will want to participate in, be it as a volunteer or an actual contributor. This "cause" is one close to your heart, and working on the project will allow you great satisfaction from watching the gift of giving at work by your own hand.

Reversed: This card indicates a shortage of sympathy and benevolence in you, usually towards one specific person or situation. Try to set aside your anger long enough to rethink your reasoning. Your judgement may be overly harsh and guided by rumor instead of fact. Make sure you have your information straight, and try a little forgiveness. It will not only help heal the situation, but your own heart.

Personal Notes

Hawthorn

Gender: Male
Planet: Mars
Element: Fire
Magical Association:
Fertility, joy

Folklore/History

In Greek and Roman times, this flower was often used as decoration at wedding feasts and on baby cradles as a symbol of hope for the future. Glastonbury Abbey is famed to have a hawthorn in bloom every Yule morning. This legend stemmed from Joseph of Arimathea and the quest for the Grail. Lore tells us that Joseph brought the sacred cup to the Abbey, and planted his staff in the ground there, from which a great hawthorn blossomed.

In recent years, scientists have begun to believe the petals may have a mild medicinal quality for lowering blood pressure. The berries and flowers of the hawthorn can also be used in tincture form as a gargle, and the blossoms especially are nice for compotes, syrup, and jelly. To make a hawthorn cordial, cover two cups of flowers with brandy and one-quarter cup of sugar. Let sit until the flowers turn translucent (one to two days), then strain and bottle.

In mystical realms, the hawthorn has been known to decorate may poles, be carried in sachets for luck, or be an integral part of the magical garden to help attract fays.

Interpretation

Upright: The language of flowers takes its cue from early days and ascribes the hawthorn to hope and marriage. For the purposes of an oracle, it might better be interpreted aspirations, wishes, and union. The union may or may not be of an emotional nature, however; it could be a new unity of thought and purpose, a oneness in your local group, or even improved office relations. Whatever the case, the accord somehow relates directly to a desire you have held in your heart for a very long time. Your waiting is about to pay off.

  Reversed: The hawthorn counsels not to spend too much time hoping for things, specifically relationships. Completely immersing yourself in daydreaming about the "perfect mate" often means you will miss the real opportunity when it presents itself. Likewise in other matters, the hawthorn cautions us against having ambitions which are too lofty and without foundation in reality. Striving for the brass ring is fine, as long as you have the building blocks you need to eventually reach it.

Personal Notes

Hazel

Gender: Male
Planet: Sun
Element: Air
Magical Association:
Luck, divination, protection vs.
storms, fulfillment of wishes,
fertility (the nut)

Folklore/History

The hazel appears in the ninth month of the Celtic tree calendar. Its branches are best known for their use as divining rods, with some suspicions that the rod of Moses may have actually been made from hazel. Hazel staffs were known to the Celtic bishops too, and in this sense they were a mark of spiritual leadership. Deities associated with the hazel are Artemis, Thor, and Diana.

Amulets made from hazel nuts are created to impart the wearer with wisdom and productive ideas, and are an appropriate charm for men wishing to improve their fecundity.

Interpretation

Upright: Reconciliation with a person or a specific situation is close at hand. While the clouds may have loomed for quite some time, new information is going to allow people to reconsider harsh words or judgements. While you may have felt somewhat persecuted, an apology is definitely in sight if you can be patient a little longer. When it does come, try and accept it graciously, and allow forgiveness to become a healing salve which makes something good out of bad circumstances. This is powerful magic!

Reversed: A difficult situation is about to get worse. The feeling behind this card is rather like having "foot-in-mouth" disease. No matter what you say or do, it seems to get garbled and tempers burn fierce. The counsel of this card is to know when you can speak effectively and when to remain still. Sometimes in the quiet we find our greatest answers … you may not have been listening to your own best advisor: your heart.

Personal Notes

Heather

Gender: Feminine
Planet: Venus
Element: Water
Magical Association:
Protection, rain magic, long
life, beauty, luck

Folklore/History

As so aptly put by Robert Louis Stevenson, "from the bonny bells of heather they brewed a drink langsyne," heather was a favored flower of the sixth-century Picts for making ale and honey.

Legend has it that if you wish to be beautiful, you should bathe in heather water once a year by the light of a full moon. However, a more practical application for this lore might be to make some heather soap for your shower. To do so, mix three-fourths cup of lye with two cups of water. Be careful with this mixture as it will give off fumes and be very hot. This must cool to the point where the container is comfortable to the touch.

At this point, slowly mix the lye and water with six cups of warm vegetable oil. As you do, it will start looking milky-white and thicken slightly. Once the lye and oil are well incorporated, you can blend in a cup of dried, ground heather flowers. If you are preparing the soap for ritual baths, this is also the best time to add any type of magical chant, incantation, etc.

Pour this entire mixture into a wooden box which has been soaked in water and lined with damp linen. On the surface of the fabric, sprinkle essential heather oil for improved scent, then lay a heavy piece of cloth over the whole box and let it cool undisturbed for twenty-four hours. The next day you can loosen the soap from its mold and cut into squares which should be allowed to age for at least three weeks before using. The longer the soap sits, the better it will lather.

This recipe can be changed for any scent, simply by substituting alternative flowers, fruit rinds, and oils.

Interpretation

Upright: Drawing the heather signifies a need in your life for some peace and quiet. You have been surrounded by people, busyness, and/or pressure for some time and really need to get away, if only in a figurative sense. A long walk in the woods, time on a deserted beach, a weekend at a hotel, a night home with the phone turned off, or a long drive would do you a world of good right now. Allow yourself to be reconnected to the natural world and the simplicity it offers to grant a moment of harmony amidst the chaos.

Reversed: The heather is a caution against too much solitude. Everyone needs privacy, but too much aloneness is not healthy. While you may be somewhat hermetic in nature, sometimes coming out of our seclusion for fellowship is needed to grow and re-energize. No one is an island, so don't be afraid to reach out. You're likely to find a hand already waiting and reaching back.

Personal Notes

Juniper

Gender: Male
Planet: Sun
Element: Fire
Magical Association:
Preservation, love, health, safety

Folklore/History

The best known use for the juniper is in the preparation of gin, whose name derives from the eighteenth century Dutch word *jenever* which means juniper! Besides this use, the leaves and berries make a good poultice or bath to ease general aches, bruises, and mild wounds.

The juniper yields yellow and green flowers, but these are not used as much as the berries which can also be added sparingly to salads or made into a marinade for game. To give your barbecued meats a lightly smoked flavor, place a few juniper branches on the coals while you cook.

Interpretation

Upright: The bows of the juniper are indicative of protection and sanctuary. In the midst of a storm, be it emotional or spiritual, something will come to break the clouds momentarily. Most likely a friend or companion will find a way to ease the difficulty on a short-term basis, giving you the much needed opportunity to re-evaluate this whole situation under less pressure. Use this time wisely by reorganizing, re-evaluating your priorities, adjusting your budget, etc. so you can handle these circumstances with a clear head and heart.

Reversed: This card can have two distinct meanings depending on other cards that appear in the spread. First, it may portend a period of feeling totally exposed to the criticisms and reproach of your family or other close group of people. This difficulty is not necessarily of your own making, so don't be afraid to stand up for your decisions if you really feel they're right.

Secondly this card may indicate a period of confusion or embarrassment coming to an end. Like a gentle sigh of relief, a new wind has come and things will soon be on the upswing.

Personal Notes

Myrtle

Gender: Feminine
Planet: Mercury/Venus
Element: Water
Magical Association:
Peace, prosperity, youthful
attitudes, guidance, improved
relationships

Folklore/History

Created by Venus and offered to Aphrodite, the myrtle has since become a very proper plant for bridal bouquets and decorations. In ancient Athens, it was the symbol of the magistrate's office, and was so popular that one-quarter of the market was devoted to making myrtle garlands. Because of this, the myrtle might also be well used in magic concerning good leadership decisions.

Interpretation

Upright: The appearance of myrtle upright in a spread indicates devotion to a cause or individual through which you gain respect. Here, your enthusiasm and unblemished zeal are soon to become contagious, so don't give up just yet. Even people who might have initially found fault with your "project" or approach will suddenly give you support and a well-deserved pat on the back. While the distinction bestowed by this situation is temporary, it will be a long-lasting memory for you, and one worth cherishing.

Reversed: The myrtle can indicate that you are chasing after a pipe dream or have set goals which are unattainable under the present circumstances. Despite warnings from more experienced people around you, you seem resolute to follow this course. While consistency and determination may be good attributes, obstinacy is not. More than likely you are hesitant to admit your mistake because it would bring a loss of face or deflate your pride. However, if you don't reconsider your approach now, the ultimate outcome of this predicament will be even more embarrassing. Remember mistakes can help us to learn, and a little humility never hurt anyone.

Personal Notes

Oak

Gender: Male
Planet: Sun
Element: Fire
Magical Association:
Protection, strength, potency,
luck, ward against illness (carry
leaf)

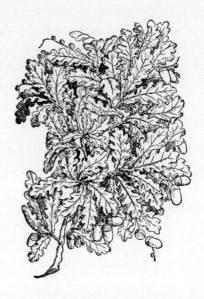

Folklore/History

The Greeks and Romans dedicated this tree to Jupiter and Zeus because of its long life and impressive bows. Other associated deities include Pan, Herne, Thor, and Diana. The Greek oracles frequently would pronounce divinations as interpreted by the rustling of oak leaves. In Rome, crowns of oak leaves were given to honored guests and the Druids derived their name from the Celtic *deru* meaning oak.

Because of their high tannin content, oak leaves make a good astringent. In decoction form, it will ease a sore throat or can be applied externally to swollen glands. The acorns of this tree can be roasted and ground for a coffee. In fact, acorn coffee was the national beverage in Germany during World War I, and it even aids digestion.

Sawdust from oak wood makes a good base for magical incense.

Interpretation

Upright: The oak represents hospitality. Days of entertaining, unexpected guests, and celebration are coming close in succession right now. This is a little bit of positive karma returning to you by way of friends, fellowship, and fun. While you have to play host/ess, it is actually enjoyable to share your abundance right now. Your courtesy will be viewed very favorably by those who stop by, and will not be forgotten in times of need.

Reversed: The need for privacy, almost to the point of hibernation, seems to pervade your mood. Something has happened which induces the desire for retreat or regrouping, like the turtle returning to its shell. This is not necessarily the best way to handle these circumstances. Hiding in the shadows does not make problems go away. Come the light of day, they will still be there. It is alright to take a temporary hiatus to regain your focus, but don't give in to the temptation to stay alone. Wrap your strength about you and meet life head on, allowing your friends to give emotional support as needed.

Personal Notes

Pine

Gender: Male
Planet: Mars
Element: Air
Magical Association:
Purification, cleansing, joy,
healing, long life, productivity

Folklore/History

When you take a walk in a pine-filled woods, you cannot help but feel refreshed. In ancient times, needles of this tree were often scattered on the floor to remove negative influences. The wood was also highly valued as a base for incense and building material.

Today the pine has found its way into numerous medicines as a bronchial disinfectant, and for inhalations for head cold and sinuses. For the latter, all you need to do is add fresh pine to a bowl of steaming water and inhale as you would over a vaporizer.

Interpretation

Upright: The flower of the evergreen is also its seed: a simple cone. Yet in this simplicity is much hidden potential. The upright figure of the pine cone speaks to you of developing your sense of self-worth. Stop looking so much at the negative that you impede all the good you can do. We tend to be our own worst critics, which is sometimes helpful, but let it be constructive criticism that builds you up within and fortifies the soul.

The only tree which stays green in winter, the evergreen is a standing emblem of vitality. Along these lines, a wintery time may be transpiring for people around you. They seem to be looking to you for hope, and a fresh wellspring of energy will be granted to you to meet this need. This is an opportunity to reaffirm your own value to yourself while helping others.

Reversed: This card warns of being falsely "puffed up," usually in regard to a specific circumstance. Before patting yourself on the back, take a second look to see who else helped you with your success, then give credit where credit is due. You will find that you gain more respect in the long run, and your achievement will be no less important.

Inverted the pine can also be advising to take special care of your physical well-being right now. Your personal energy could be waning, so watch what you eat, get plenty of rest, and don't over extend yourself to tasks that could wait.

Personal Notes

Poplar

Gender: Feminine
Planet: Saturn
Element: Water
Magical Association:
Improving spirits, financial
matters

Folklore/History

The famed balm of Gilead is part of the poplar's family tree. In earlier times, the bark was often used as a quinine substitute for treating fevers, the tincture acting like aspirin. Modern uses include adding poplar buds to certain cosmetics to guard against rancidity, and for creams to treat burns.

Interpretation

Upright: The poplar is the signpost of time's passage. It may indicate a coming of age, the ending of an initiatory period, or any number of other significant transitions in one's life. This card usually indicates a cycle coming to an end. For the student, he or she will go on to graduation and college or a job. For the parent, a child will leave home for the first time.

These types of changes are both exhilarating and frightening. You cannot help but be pleased by the new maturity evidenced, yet letting go of the past is not always easy. Now is the time to review the foundations you have built to make certain they can withstand the times yet to be. Once confident in that knowledge, you can forge into your future with surety.

Reversed: Uprooted, the poplar indicates instead of the end of a long road, the beginning of one. A pregnancy could occur at an unexpected time, a metaphysical teacher could be found to guide you in totally unfamiliar realms, or you could start a new but uncertain job.

Not unlike the upright card, beginnings can be just as confusing emotionally. Just when things seemed to be settling down, these unforeseen circumstances tend to leave your best laid plans in disarray. The best suggestion from this card is to pick up the mess, and re-sort it with your new situation in mind. This is an opportunity to re-learn organizational skills and flexibility. Flow with the moment instead of getting washed away.

Personal Notes

Willow

Gender: Feminine
Planet: Moon
Element: Water
Magical Association:
Protection, healing, love, death,
moon magic

Folklore/History

Associated with Hera, Hecate, and Ceres, the willow represents the Crone aspect of the Goddess. It has been associated with magic for hundreds of years because its pliant branches act as a reminder of what true magic is: a bending of energy. Willow is a favored wood for witches' brooms.

Ancient charms against fever were made from willow branches, and Dioscorides recommended willow bark frequently in the treatment of pain as do many tribal cultures.

In America, willows were first introduced by Anglican missionaries who were aware of the bark's aspirin-like qualities. To make a decoction, take one teaspoon of bark to one and a half pints of water and boil for thirty minutes. This preparation can also act as a skin astringent.

Interpretation

Upright: The willow usually is considered the tree of mourning, and thus it weeps. When this card appears in your spread, it is the sign of sorrow or drastic changes which cause emotional upheaval. Now is a good time to call in your favors and turn to supportive friends. You cannot be the proverbial port in the sorm all the time. Rely on those you trust and love to help give you strength to endure the days ahead. Time will heal these wounds, as will a little TLC from those you have so frequently given care to in the past. Don't allow your stubborn will to get in the way of help that you need now.

Reversed: A time of mourning is over and the clouds have begun to move away with great relief. You may feel as if you have awakened from a long sleep and finally have the perspective to cope with life again. As trite as it may seem, it is during these storms that we often find our greatest strength and grow as people. Take a deep breath and be thankful for what has passed, and what is yet to come.

Personal Notes

Woodruff

Gender: Male
Planet: Mars
Element: Fire
Magical Association:
Victory, financial matters,
spring rituals

Folklore/History

Germans call it *waldmeister*, meaning "master of the woods," and it grows in great abundance on the Rhine. Fifteenth-century churches used it to decorate the rafters as a means of protection, especially from various insects.

Described as carrying the scent of hay and vanilla, it is the prime magical ingredient for many a May wine. To make an easy version, pour cider over fresh woodruff which is iced. Let stand for thirty minutes. Next melt two ounces of sugar into one-quarter pint of water and mix with the rest of the ingredients, removing the woodruff. Add a slice of orange and enjoy. Woodruff may also be used in soups, sauces, salads, and teas.

Interpretation

Upright: Modest worth is predicted by this card. You may be cleaning out your attic, helping with a garage sale, or some similar activity, and have an item really catch your eye. Don't ignore it. This is the whimsy part of fate sparkling a little luck your way. The item will not be a rare gem or painting, but resale will net you a tidy profit if you are shrewd but honest.

Reversed: You have been sold a line of goods, and are now stuck with low-quality junk. Depending on the cost of this situation, you may wish to take consumer action. However, if it is only minor in nature, you can file it in the "wiser for the experience" folder, and go get something from a reputable source to replace it.

Personal Notes

Yew

Gender: Feminine
Planet: Venus
Element: Water
Magical Association:
Resurrection, beginnings

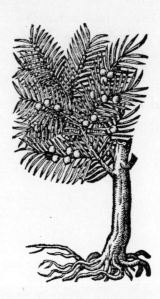

Folklore/History

A famous feature in Old-World gardens, this member of the pine family is recognized by its lush, velvety foliage. Some of these stately trees have obtained heights of one hundred feet with trunks ten feet around.

The yew is the sacred tree of India, and is burned as incense in many temples. The English and Native Americans alike valued it for its resilience, making it the favored wood for longbows. The dark version of the yew tree is considered the symbol of life after death and is favored for churchyards. Beneath its branches is also a preferred mourning place for unhappy lovers.

Interpretation

Upright: Renewed vision, faith, and a whole new lease on life are indicated by the appearance of this card, especially in the outcome position of a spread. Like a phoenix, you are born anew with creative ideas, inspiration, and actually feel like a new person. Something you have done for yourself is to thank for these wonderful perspectives. Maybe you started an exercise program, are eating well-rounded meals, or taking up yoga and sufi dancing. Whatever the activity, keep doing it! The very fibers of your being are refreshed in the process.

Reversed: The yew counsels that something you have longed for may not come to pass. A wedding could be canceled, or an important project which has been central to your planning could fall through. In this case, the message of the yew is twofold. First, the alteration may only be temporary in nature; just long enough to be certain attitudes and desires are what they should be. A period of self-examination is definitely called for. Second, if the ending is a permanent one, there is a good reason for it. It may take time to recognize the "whys," but when you do, you will be able to cope with the disappointment much better.

Personal Notes

Alternative Trees

The following trees were included in some of the lists of flower languages and not in others. Since many of them may be useful to your personal magical work, especially as spell or incense components, or for alternatives in your oracle, I have shared them here as an added reference.

Cedar: Inner capabilities, purification and cleansing, auric work, wholeness of body or spirit.

Dogwood: Meetings and communication, wishes.

Elm: The ability to overcome faults and make them strengths.

Fig: Enlightenment, awakening the intuitive and feminine natures, releasing blockages, enhancing creative forces within.

Maple: Equilibrium, grounding of magical energy, ambitions.

Redwood: Time's passage, immutableness, outlooks, inventiveness, tranquility.

Rowan: The senses, discernment, safety, acquiring familiars, Goddess energy, muse, vision, elemental guidance.

Sandalwood: Meditation, divination, self-confidence in matters of spiritual path and teachings.

Suggested Sources for Trees

- If you explain that you are doing a "botanical" project, frequently arboretums and greenhouses will allow you to get a leaf or other small bit of the tree you need. They will also often have pamphlets with pictures you could use.

- Your local park often has a wide variety of trees. To identify them, check a field guide to trees and bushes. Some bird watching books include this information.

- Nature publications such as *National Geographic* often have beautiful pictures which you can photocopy or cut out and use.

⁊ If you are fortunate enough to live in the country or are able to travel there, take a nature walk to see what surprises are in store.

⁊ Check your local lawn and garden shops. These places have special tags they use for identifying trees and will frequently offer to give you some if you ask politely. These tags usually have a photograph.

CHAPTER SEVEN

Alternative Symbols for Oracles

But soon within that mirror huge and high,
was seen a self-emitted light to gleam.

Sir Walter Scott

The accurate prophet or diviner gathers impressions from a source normally untouched by humankind. Some believe this ability is due to predestination; the notion that all things in life are foreordained. Others postulate that there is a gift within certain individuals that responds almost like a seismograph to the ever-changing current of events leading to the future. No matter what the ascribed theory, however, it is a fact that divinatory practices have existed in wide and varied forms throughout the world as is evidenced clearly in written history.

In Appendix A you will find a brief list of some of these methods along with their "technical" names. Besides those given, other interesting forms of prophesy have included the use of feathers, butter lamps, bones, and shells! It seems from this observation, that each culture and its intricate factions have somehow found a way to effect a divination system reflective of their society, locale, myths, and religious teachings.

Because of the individual nature of the soul, we could potentially expect that everyone on this planet would desire a completely different system based on temperament. In much the same manner, it would be naive of me to assume everyone reading this book would find a basic Victorian oracle satisfactory to their personal needs or outlooks. With this in mind, I would like to propose some alternative approaches for you to try not only for yourself, but perhaps as a gift for a friend. These options may be used as an *enhancement* to the language of flowers, by themselves, or in any combination thereto.

Base Mediums

We have already talked about the use of wood slices, beach stone, and art paper or cardboard as the foundation for a divinatory tool, but there are many other options. Simple prophetic tools can be found in items such as sand, flour, baby powder, dry earth, or rice, which can be cast on a slightly damp surface to see what patterns emerge. In this case, you concentrate on your question, dust the surface with your chosen "tool," then observe the results. The interpretation can be based on your own intuition or the significance of the emblem perceived as given in the lists which follow later in this chapter.

For more precise techniques, many other mediums can act as your base. These include clay, crystals, similar sized sticks (specifically for Wittan wands—used in an ancient form of Celtic divination), various types of soft metals such as brass and silver (best for runes), shells, stiffened canvas (for card base), beans (which can either be used either for their numerical significance or be marked with symbols), etc.

The above inventory is really only a starting point. When you have a few minutes someday, try taking another look around your own home with the goal of making a divination tool in mind. I think you will be pleasantly surprised by the number of items you can find which could conceivably function as segments of your creative project.

The Symbols

Even if you are using the most simple divination techniques, symbolism and associated interpretations are central to this mystical art; be it the symbols you want to choose from to adorn your instrument, or those which appear during the readings.

Since most people will probably choose a system which will allow for a greater variety of personalized interpretations, I would like to share some of the emblems which have commonly been used for creating and explicating oracles throughout history. If you are employing a simple form of divination, such as the casting mentioned earlier, you can use these lists as a guideline, along with your intuition, to discern what your resulting symbols mean.

On the other hand, if you are implementing them to create an elective oracle, I suggest you either use only one list, or combinations of lists which are consistent and compatible. While mixing many different metaphorical figures might offer greater diversity, historically speaking divinatory devices have usually had some type of thematic undercurrent. The end result is that the converging composition binds the individual symbols together so that the whole, completed tool functions cohesively, like a well-formed team.

This particular method of motif is perhaps best evidenced in almost every Tarot deck presently on the market. Each one has sought out a particular central focus, to which the basic elements of coins, cups, wands, and swords are added along with color representations. It is this type of well-blended structure that you are hoping to achieve in your oracle.

As you choose your theme and related emblems, you can then decide how to best illustrate them on your background. Many of the techniques shared for the language of flowers (carving, painting, and decoupage) are equally useful for these alternative approaches. Whatever you finally select, take your time and write down your interpretations of each before, during, and after they are completed. Believe it or not, the explanation may change for you during the origination process because of the amount of concentration you give to the individual designs. Also be sure to note your ideas for spreads or castings (see Chapter Two). While this is a little time consuming, the added bonus is that your written guide for readings will be completed in the same period as the oracle itself.

For the purpose of simplicity, I have given some suggested interpretations of the listed symbols in *upright* positions. To apply the reversed meaning of the card, try considering antonyms to the readings given. For example, if the number one appears inverted in your spread, it could portend procrastination and the inability to act on your dreams. Please remember that these are only proposals, which can and should be changed to better represent your Path and ideals.

Remember, too, that this is a learning experience to be enjoyed on that level. You are about to re-examine your feelings about the future, about today, about your personal symbolisms and ideologies. Because of this introspection, the invention process offers you a tremendous opportunity for personal growth.

Again, I would like to stress that you do not have to be incredibly talented to make a magical tool which will perform very well for you. The Great Spirit, while appreciative of individual gifts, looks at the heart of the matter. If you develop a divinatory system with the correct intentions and endow it with your best effort, then the results cannot help but be positive.

Animals

The use of animals as symbols is very old. Mostly, animals were used in divination by signs and omens, their movements and activities being considered messages by those in observance. The most popular animal, by far, for this type of oracle has been the bird. Among the Hittites, as early as 1330 B.C., a system of interpreting twenty-seven different species of birds and their activities was devised. In German and Norse countries, the crow, eagle, and raven were focused on for divine missives.

For the purpose of your personal oracle, you may wish to use the feathers or fur of a particular creature (with permission from the animal, of course) or a picture representation. As you choose your images, consider the position the animal has taken for a stance. This bearing can be very useful to your final decision regarding the reading's interpretation. For example, a sleeping dog might be deciphered as peaceful service, while one with its ears up could portend cautious alert.

Ant: Persistence, a knowing that what is yours will eventually come to you, a period where you must trust in a specific individual or set of circumstances.

Bear: Thoughtfulness, a period of rest or retreat, visions, the intuitive nature, strongly asserted truths.

Beaver: The perpetual doer, matters pertaining to building, protecting, action, solutions, and service.

Bee: Pleasure, cultivation, caution against getting "stung," element of Air, busy matters.

Beetle: New life, authenticity, regeneration, strength, courage, the sun's power.

Butterfly: Element of Air, human spirit or soul, metamorphosis and change, lifting of burdens.

Cat: Balance, natural power, timelessness, grace in motion.

Crow: The principles of the universe vs. those of humankind, speaking out against injustice or atrocity, integrity of word and deed.

Deer: Compassion, love without conditions, gentleness, the hunt, alertness.

Dog: Service to others, faithfulness, devotion, the ability to listen closely without judgement.

Dolphin: Ecology, element of Water, bliss, spiritual growth, deliverance, the breath of life.

Dove: Seers and prophets, redemption, purity, safe havens, peace.

Dragonfly: Dreams, fortune, ancient remembrance and power, the art of the mystic, elements of Air and Fire.

Eagle: Fresh perspectives, ability to rise above circumstances, self-healing, symmetry, tests, getting rid of illusions.

Fish: Good luck, prosperity, satisfaction, serenity.

Fox: Adaptation, confidence in the future, quickness of response, the ability to become invisible.

Frog: Cleansing, fluidity, rejuvenation, purging.

Hawk: Examination, signals, attitudes, intuition, concern for details.

Horse: Messenger of the gods, the wise use of power, understanding, any matters pertaining to movement.

Hummingbird: Duality, flexibility, mirth, passion for beauty, the essence of life, bursts of energy, insight, or power.

Lion: Solar energy, metaphysical aspects of humankind, watchfulness, preservation.

Lizard: Messages (especially divine ones), dreams, swiftness, fears, hopes, symmetry.

Mouse: Close examination, methodology, approaching a matter with concern for detail, prudence.

Otter: Playfulness, potency of pure joy, elements of Earth and Water, healthy inquisitiveness.

Owl: The ancient secrets, wisdom, truth, perspicacity to see beyond the surface, clairvoyance.

Peacock: Comeliness, ambition, shrewdness, eternity, sometimes false self-esteem.

Phoenix: Resurrection, new beginnings, drastic transformation, the element of Fire.

Porcupine: The strength of faith and trust, the ability to get past superficial matters.

Rabbit: Work on the things that you can change and stop worrying about things you cannot. Fear is a strong enemy, don't let it overcome you.

Raven: Bearer of energy, changes in awareness, the magical spark being awakened, mysticism.

Scorpion: Initiation, clarification, inception or creation (especially of a spiritual disposition).

Skunk: Reverence, the power of self-belief and assertion, circumstances relating to your personal reputation.

Snake: Self-knowledge for boon or bane, growth, transformation, development, sensuality, elements of Fire and Earth.

Spider: Networking, trickery, the fates, time's passage, the future, energies of originality.

Squirrel: Preparation for change, scarcity, getting rid of any excess burdens in your life. Center attention on home and personal needs.

Swan: Develop your intuitive sense and respect your instincts. A reminder that beauty is within, as well as transformational power.

Turtle: Long life, the world's movements, sanctuary, slow but steady progress, feminine attributes, foundations.

Unicorn: Insight, childlike purity and innocence, defense of those who are vulnerable.

Whale: Ancient wisdom, the Crone, elements of Air and Water, clairaudience, telepathy, universal understanding, languages.

Wolf: The ability to track or guide through the present confusions, strong sense of family or group belonging, aptitude for participating yet remaining individual, increases in psychic energy and new ideas.

Suggested Sources for Animals

- Your local veterinarian may have illustrated pamphlets on various animals.

- Zoos often provide books and guides. Don't forget your camera!

- Children's coloring books and educational guides.

- Old encyclopedias, postcards, and posters.

- Nature hikes can often produce startling results. You will frequently find feathers or bits of fur caught in a thorny tree. Periodically you can get real fur bits at a secondhand store, if that's what you would like to use.

Personal Notes

Astrology

The earliest surviving horoscope is from Babylon 410 B.C. By 300 B.C., in the same region, astrological arts had been refined to the point where each sign had twelve subdivisions. Mesopotamian priests connected the sun, moon, and planets with a god or goddess, believing that each represented an orderly structure of the universe. Astrology in scientific form, however, followed later on the heels of astronomy.

Popular first in primarily the Greek speaking world, astrology's principle philosophies were laid by Aristotle. During his life he spoke of heavenly bodies as being responsible for promoting actions on Earth. Greek physician Galen (130-201 A.D.) strongly believed in the validity of this idea, adding that signs such as meteors, lightning, etc. must also be considered. Other herbalists in the Middle Ages also advocated this theory.

This connection of the living world to the movements of the universe faded momentarily during the Age of Reason, but by 1930 was seeing a substantial refreshed interested in the United States and abroad. While most of this interest in the planets and signs centered around daily guides or planting cycles, pictures of the planets and their symbols or zodiacal signs could be added to your oracle to aid interpretations.

If you choose to use these emblems in any way, you can further enhance the potency of each by working during that planetary or zodiacal phase. To know when these occur, consult a good astrological guide such as *Llewellyn's Daily Planetary Guide* which is produced annually.

Planets

Mercury: Symbol ☿; matters of communication, speed, logic and reason, integrating lessons of any kind.

Venus: Symbol ♀; sense of attraction, love, joy, all elements of social graces.

Earth: Symbol ⊕; the home and family, ecology, foundations, grounding.

Mars: Symbol ♂; force, vitality, sexuality, momentum, direction, focus, manifestation in particular.

Jupiter: Symbol ♃; growth, ethical circumstances, a knowledge of your relationship to the universe, tact, karmic law, matters of health.

Saturn: Symbol ♄; structure, attitudes, stability, freedom from some type of dependency.

Uranus: Symbol ♅; mental liberation, ability to act on your dreams, inspiration, humor, the child within.

Neptune: Symbol ♆; a broadened vision, change from being bored, the ability to dream is being awakened, artistic vision refreshed.

Pluto: Symbol ♇; preservation of culture or life, humanitarian efforts, procreation, refreshed love for fellow people.

Zodiacal Signs

Aries: Symbol ♈; March 21st-April 21st; a Fire sign which is full of courage and lively energy. Excellent for leadership and instruction.

Taurus: Symbol ♉; April 21st-May 21st; an Earth sign which has a strong love of beauty. Any matters pertaining to compassion, the arts, or sensibility.

Gemini: Symbol ♊; May 21st-June 21st; an Air sign pertaining to matters of the mind, specifically scholastic endeavors and adaptability.

Cancer: Symbol ♋; June 21st-July 21st; a Water sign full of whimsy, adventure, romance, and determination.

Leo: Symbol ♌; July 21st-August 21st; a Fire sign which embodies many masculine attributes including strength, fortitude, and valor.

Virgo: Symbol ♍; August 21st-September 21st; an Earth sign concerning matters of humor, practicality, discernment, and insight.

Libra: Symbol ♎; September 21st-October 21st; an Air sign which pertains to matters of agreement, fairness, resolutions, and viewpoints.

Scorpio: Symbol ♏; October 21st-November 21st; a Water sign that is full of intense power, especially of an emotional nature. It also applies to situations where discrepancy exists.

Sagittarius: Symbol ♐; November 21st-December 21st; a Fire sign attributed to items of will, respect, patience, and honesty.

Capricorn: Symbol ♑; December 21st-January 21st; an Earth sign symbolizing persistence, hard work, goals, and diligence.

Aquarius: Symbol ♒; January 21st-February 21st; an Air sign characterizing generosity, empathy, discernment, idealism, and charity.

Pisces: Symbol ♓; February 21st-March 21st; a Water sign of love, persistence, imagination, and foresight.

Personal Notes

Colors

There are many portions of our mind not commonly reached by daily activity. Colors allow us to quickly apply their ascribed characteristics to our magical attempts because they appeal to our sense of vision, both inside and out. One such example might be found with pale blue. It is easy to look at, often bringing to mind a clear sky or calm ocean. Because of this it has a mild tranquilizing effect on most people, helping to bring relaxation when exposed to the hue over periods of time.

For your divinatory device, just consider what first comes to mind when you think of a particular shade. This initial response, if noted, will be very helpful to your creative use of the color. For example, if you think of yellow as pertaining to prophesy, it might be the ideal background pigment for your oracle. Or, if green makes you feel lively and spirited, you might want to incorporate it into the symbol pertaining to personal energy in your system.

Black: In some traditions, protection. Alternatively sickness, tension, "dark clouds," brooding, night and dreaming, our personal specters, grieving, endings. Energy to absorb negativity or turn around undesired circumstances. An understanding of human nature. Restraint.

Blue: Connected with the element of Water, this is a peaceful tone which portends inspiration, wholeness, and rejuvenation. Attributes of understanding, devotion, sincerity, and affection. It is also frequently associated with art, creativity, humanitarian efforts, and moodiness.

Brown: Survival skills, grounding, working with the land.

Gold: Universal life energy, the color of the sun, masculine attributes, quick actions, money, legal matters.

Green: The elements of Earth and Water, a part of growth and a sign of harvest to efforts well done. Also good for money-related symbolism, anything pertaining to nature, luck, fertility, confidence, healing, and hope.

Grey: Total neutrality and balance.

Orange: Warmth, companionship, abundance, and the element of Fire. Good for any token which deals with prosperity, fellowship, and social occasions. Mental agility in action, encouragement, adaptation, kindness, strength of character.

Purple: A color of power and psychic pursuits, calming and refreshing, usually spiritual in nature. Also associated with ambition, progress, self-assurance, and intelligence.

Red: The waters of life run red and because of this it is associated with intensity, emotions, peril, and power. This is also a hue of drastic change, strength, clarity, and pure love. It may also be connected with the aggressive nature of humankind.

White: Reconciliation, harmony, forgiveness, used almost universally as the color of protection and positive magic. The full moon aspect of the Goddess, purity, perfection, heart-felt spiritual goals.

Yellow: Charm and excitement, increasing energy and inspiration. Matters pertaining to mental learning, comfort, triumph. Frequently affiliated with friendly natures and curiosity.

Personal Notes

Stones and Metals

Many types of precious and semiprecious stones have been used as talismans in ancient and modern civilizations. In terms of divination practices, however, crystals are better known as aids to fortunetellers through the technique of scrying. "Scrying" comes from the English word *descry* which means discover.

Depending on the medium, a flame or clouds may appear and form images in the crystal, which are then interpreted accordingly. Studies were done on scrying techniques in the late nineteenth and early twentieth century. Generally the belief is that the individual brings on a self-induced trance or such absorption in the work that he or she notices nothing else.

For the purpose of a personal oracle, you can use crystals in this manner, or you can utilize them as a base material, concurrent to your inclinations, to which other symbols can be added by way of carving, painting, or gluing. If the actual stone is unavailable due to supply or cost, you may feel free to substitute an item of similar color instead.

Agate: Situations involving the weather or your personal ability to gain perspective.

Amber: Increased energy, sometimes thought to be a dwelling for spirits, capture or arrested motion.

Amethyst: Controlling negative thoughts or habits, making ingenious judgments, victory, protection.

Aquamarine: Matters of courage or bravery in decision making.

Beryl: Friendship, vitality, keenness of mind, refreshing the feelings of love in a close relationship.

Bloodstone: Protection of life, recognition of your efforts along those lines, wisdom gained through experience.

Carnelian: Fortune, safety, honor, opportunity, effective powers of speech.

Chrysolite: Protection from things that dwell in the shadows, banishing undesired energy and restoring personal vitality.

Copper: Conduction and stabilization.

Coral: Settling thoughts or confusions, increased stamina, bringing wisdom into your life, the creative power of the sea.

Diamond: Clarity of thought and intentions, strength and endurance, modesty and purity.

Emerald: Romance, joy, unity in the home, quieting storms (especially of an emotional nature), vision for the future.

Gold: Earthly fortunes, masculine powers, the sun's energy.

Gypsum: Protection, innocence, destiny, good luck, success (Hematite), accomplishment and mastery especially with regard to a legal matter.

Iron: Connected to the element of Earth, implies strength, durability, and an unyielding position on a particular matter of opinion.

Jade: Productivity, healing, romance, longevity, protection (especially of children).

Jasper: Turning a negative situation around, controlling your fears, weather control.

Lapis Lazuli: Psychic protector, clear-mindedness, protection from trauma, a remedy for melancholy.

Lead: Foundations, possibly slowness of decision making or action in a specific situation.

Lodestone: Morality, true devotion, might, the ability to draw people or things into your life through magical means.

Malachite: Health and well-being (especially related to children and their protection).

Moonstone: Good fortune (especially in love) as well as the traditionally ascribed attributes of the moon (specifically feminine power, spiritual wisdom, awareness).

Obsidian: Control over your spiritual energy and direction of power.

Onyx: A special token of friendship or connections in a relationship.

Ruby: Matters of the heart (especially sadness).

Sapphire: Faithfulness, sincerity, devotion (specifically with regard to your spiritual path), divine favor.

Silver: The moon in all its phases, aspect of the Goddess, peacefulness.

Tin: Luck and fate.

Turquoise: Protection (especially from falling or devastating circumstances), timeliness, healing, bringing guardian animal spirits into your life.

Suggested Sources for Stones and Metals

- Science hobby stores.
- Geology departments at local colleges.
- New Age and magical stores.
- Gem and mineral shows.
- Lapidaries.

In all these cases, don't forget to shop around! Many of these people will be able to give you other contacts too, or recommend alternative resources for pictures of the stones you wish to use.

Personal Notes

Numbers

Thousands of year ago, Pythagoras proposed that every letter and number somehow exhibited clues to the mysteries of the universe. Since that time the study and use of numerology as a divination system has been widely known. From using the digits in your birthday or the quantity of letters in your name to counting the number of birds flying overhead, numerals seem to carry a mystique all their own which can be employed effectively in your oracle.

You may either place the number itself on your base medium as the symbol, or use the number in combination with other tokens for an amplified impact. For example, since heather is the flower of busy schedules and the need for a break, you might choose to place three sprigs of heather on your card, three being a number which portends similar interpretations.

1: Power, fire, the ability to be a pioneer and follow through on your dreams, determination, ambition, intense goals and energy, singularity of purpose.

2: Peace, sensitivity, mystery, social matters, affection, talent with words, the ability to balance business against art or home.

3: Creativity, change, restlessness, the art of conversation, busy schedules, responsibility, the triune nature of humanity and the divine.

4: Earth, practicality, completion, research and study, a special aptitude towards the technical, duty, balance, memory.

5: Impulsive or restless natures, challenge in new situations, unexpected or unusual meetings, friendships, sensuality.

6: Beauty, harmony, synchronicity, the union of dreams and reality, spiritual growth.

7: Philosophy and deep study, self-discipline, mental skills, timing, any situation or a secretive or reluctant nature.

8: Leadership or attention to business and finance, sense of humor to balance success.

9: Humanitarian efforts, compassion, fiery emotions, dynamics in matters of politics, desire for freedom or adventure.

10: Sudden change in fortune or fate, attention to mental nature vs. physical, worry and emotional matters.

11: Idealism, quiet, original notions, being the master of your own mind, the ability to be unswayed by others' opinions.

12: Deceptive appearances (especially in regard to your perspective of self), completed cycles.

Personal Notes

Miscellaneous Objects

Since magic should be something which grows and changes, it would be rather innocent to think that all our standards would or could endure unchanged for future generations. We live in a "brave new world" where gadgets of all kinds are quickly revolutionizing our lives. With such advances come a whole new set of emblems which can be used and interpreted for divinatory work, be it comprehending dreams or employing the emblem for part of your oracle.

With this in mind, I have listed below several symbols, both old and new, with suggested interpretations in alphabetical order. This is not a complete list, and should act as a guideline only. What you perceive as being important in your reading or experiences is the best measure of the explication you can have available to you.

Abracadabra: Considered a magical word when written in the form of a triangle, protection against sickness.

Airplane: Movement, Air element. The direction of the airplane can be significant to bringing something into your life or moving it away.

Answering Machine: Annoyance, not getting through to someone, missed connections, any communications.

Arcade Token: Temptation, distraction.

Armor: Protection, slowed movement, pending battles.

Arrow: Warning, messages, directions, the warrior spirit. An upward pointed arrow is usually a positive sign, while a downward one indicates final judgement falling.

Atom: Energy, strong bonds, change (often of a drastic nature).

Baby: Innocence, new beginnings, possible financial burdens, the need for restraint.

Balloon: Hot air, inflated ego or ideas, need to ground yourself.

Bank: Security, financial matters of any kind, savings.

Banner: A declaration, in earlier times it showed a household's protection over an individual. What is on the banner can be more significant than the flag itself.

Bar: Social interaction, secrets, deception, relationships.

Barbecue: Change, family, gatherings, element of Fire.

Basket: Surprises, leisure, good food and fellowship, fertility in the physical sense.

Basketball: Feeling jumpy, need to rise above seemingly impossible odds.

Beans: Hot air, half truths, people being two-faced.

Bed: Rest, security, sensuality.

Black Sheep: Guilt, feeling left out or uncomfortable.

Bomb: Destruction, drastic change which is frequently not positive, anger which needs control, lack of subtlety.

Book Bag: Education, study, burdens, the mind.

Boots: Indirectness, secrecy, difficult progress, protection from rough weather. Please note that the type of boots may change the interpretation slightly. For instance, boots made for rain could symbolize emotional upset and tears, while alternatively snow boots might portend the "cold shoulder."

Bottle: A full bottle is always positive (especially in matters of relationships). If it is half full, check to see what is missing. If it is empty, there is nothing good for you in this situation.

Bowl: A full bowl may be the symbol of prosperity, while an empty one portends poverty and hunger (which may be of a spiritual nature).

Brick Wall: Overlooking the obvious, lack of attention, hidden matters, blocked progress often from within.

Bridge: Overcoming difficulties, positive change, life transformations, passages, endings and beginnings.

Bubbles: Lightness, unburdened, possible warning of lack of thought or foresight.

Buddha: Meditation, contemplation, peacefulness, drawing toward Eastern mysticism.

Cake: Prosperity (sometimes at someone else's expense), dualities, selfishness, celebrations.

Calculator: Financial matters, money under scrutiny, audits, the need to verify your sources.

Calendar: Appointments, the passage of the seasons, cycles.

California: The sun's energy, free thinking, progress, need for stable foundations.

Camera: Surprise, sudden awareness, special occasions, possible entrapment, travel.

Candle: Illumination, ancient knowledge revealed, magical study, the element of Fire. The color of the candle can change its significance to your reading (see also "Colors," in this chapter).

Car: Movement, enjoyment, job. A car horn, by contrast, is often anger, noise, or blockage.

Chair (living room-style): Repose, rest, leisure.

Chess Set: Intense concentration, attention to detail, mental activity. You may use each chess piece separately for a wider variety of interpretations. For example, kings can mean power, leadership, etc., while pawns indicate some form of manipulation occurring.

Chocolate: Magic involving the senses, cravings, dietary changes, pleasurable pursuits.

Clock Radio: Anything involving time. With an alarm, it is trying to get you motivated or alert you to missed opportunity.

Closet: Seemingly embarrassing secrets, hidden matters, openings and closings.

Clothesline: The element of Air, freshness and renewal.

Computer: Focus, memory, positive use of technology.

Condom: Protection, wise choices, sexuality, modern morality.

Condominium: A modern-day castle. Watch your money flow, make sure you build on strong foundations.

Confetti: Celebration, a well-earned day off.

Crystals: See "Stones and Metals" in this chapter.

Dagger: Separation, cutting words, male energy.

Dam: Blocked or stored creativity, Water element.

Doorbell: Guests, news, alertness.

Doughnut: Distraction, attention in wrong place, fellowship.

Drawer: Storage, neatness, sense of organization.

Drum: Warnings and announcements, cycles or rhythms.

Dryer: Air element, easing burdens, light, airy feelings, freshness.

Eclipse: Obscured vision, transitions, in-between the worlds.

Electrical Outlet (lines): Power, connections.

False Teeth: Insecurity, false first impressions, something hidden or mis-represented.

Fan: Air element, refreshing, cooling off, winds of change.

Feathers: Laughter, a well-received gift, messages, honesty.

Fence: Protection, interrupted communications, privacy.

Filing Cabinet: Need for organization, cleaning out of old matters, sorting out priorities.

Fireworks: Inspiration, creativity, sensuality.

Food: It depends on the type, but they are too numerous to list here. For a good reference on this see *The Magic in Food* by Scott Cunningham (Llewellyn Publications).

Food Processor: Change of form or state, making things conform to a particular size or image.

Football: Pass on this situation or tackle it head on. Stop pussyfooting around.

Glue Gun: Quick fixes, stick-to-itiveness, repairs needed.

Grain: Prosperity, faith, sustenance.

Gun: Anger, lack of control or focus, bitterness or the possible hold up of an expected situation.

Hair Net: Constraint, restrictions, control, work.

Hair Piece: Humor, partial honesty, attention to superficials.

Hamper: Pay attention to signals which warn of gossip or the need for cleansing.

Handcuffs (binding hands): Healing work, sharing, companionship, assistance.

Hard Hat: Protection, especially for the mind.

High Heels: Change in perspective, outer appearances, festive occasions.

Hockey Puck: You are getting the short end of the stick in a situation which may be close to violent in nature. Slippery ground slows footing.

Incense: Interest in spiritual realms, meditation, quiet time.

Iron: The need to resolve a specific situation, working out the kinks in a plan.

Jug: Element of water, spiritual thirst, refreshment.

Key: Doors opening, new beginnings, movement, travel.

Keyhole: Snooping, gossip, embarrassing information, revealing secrets.

Lamp: If lit, new insights and understanding. If dark, the need for examination and rethinking your options. It might be interesting to have it each way for upright and reversed.

Lawn Mower: Cutting away the old, outgrown ideas and ways.

Lock: Closed path, places where you are not ready to go, fears.

Lottery Ticket: Temptation, luck, fate, money matters.

Meteor: Flash of inspiration, warning against using too much energy, burning out, drastic modifications.

Microfilm: Attention to detail, nit-picking, also may indicate a personal gift of Sight which needs to be developed.

Microscope: The feeling of being small or insignificant, a close examination of the self with respect to the world.

Mirror: Reflections (especially those pertaining to physical appearance), false images.

Money: Material world, security, meeting obligations.

Moon: The significance of moon phases is fairly well-known to magic. In the Tarot, the moon card represents something hidden. If waxing, the matter is coming into being; if waning, it has just passed.

Neon Light: Too much attention to self, being "starry-eyed."

Nuclear Reactor: Intense energy to the point of being dangerous, consider the motives of your magic, a reminder to use power responsibly.

Nylons: Support, appearances.

Olympic Torch: Victory, the spirit of cooperation, energy of youth, the element of Fire.

Paper Clip: Securing legal matters, holding things together but only loosely.

Parachute: A need to bail out of a situation gracefully, finding freedom, element of Air.

Pizza: Slice of life, gatherings, sharing, the wheel of fortune.

Planets: Cycles, dreams, outside influences. Each planet has slightly different ascribed meanings as discussed earlier this chapter.

Pollution: Awareness, cleansing, need to reconnect with nature.

Rain Forest: Ecology, healing Gaia, Earth-related spells, water.

Recreational Vehicle: Vacation, rest, a haven, possible travel.

Red Pen: Brooding over mistakes, self-correction or harsh correction from another.

Red Tape: No positive progress, stalling and run-arounds, any matter which pertains to delays, restriction, or binding.

Refrigerator: Preservation, sustenance, cool attitudes.

Remote Control: Power, possible manipulation, need for regulation or supervision, life on "pause."

Rocket: Exploration, rapid growth, movement.

Ruler: Measuring your life against a standard, close observation, values and allotment.

Runes: See separate listing this chapter.

Satellite Dish: Sense of hearing. If pointed away, it means you are not heeding good advice. Pointed towards you, it indicates receptiveness to new ideas.

Scales: Balance, weight loss, considering your options.

Scissors: Cut away things, negative feelings, separation, change, creativity.

Smoke: Signals, communication, health matters, cleansing.

Soap: The need to clean up your act (specifically your communication skills), time for purification and cleansing.

Space Station: Adventures, new frontiers, possibly a new job or home.

Sports Car: Life in the fast lane, a warning to slow down and watch more carefully.

Stereo Speakers: Too many opinions, need for focus and clarity. Take some time alone to listen to your own heart.

Stove: Warming matters up, home and family, entertainment, ideas baking slowly to perfection.

Suitcase: Travel, change, perspectives, adventure.

Sword: Ancient honor, fealty, pride, the warrior spirit balanced against the art of the blade.

Synthesizer: Be like the chameleon and know how to blend with your surroundings. Flexibility and change.

Tarot: Like the runes, meanings are specific to each card. The whole deck is a symbol of divination, intuition, and the focusing of psychic energy. For specific Tarot cards, refer to any deck or book on the subject.

Telescope: New horizons, new perspectives, a higher outlook for your personal and/or spiritual life, new understanding of your place in the universe, time travel.

Television: The media, distraction, the family, enjoyment.

Test Tube: Study, health, fertility, sterile atmosphere.

Tissues: Sorrow, cleansing, possible sickness.

Toothbrush: Hygiene, care of self, cleansing.

Trash Can: Waste, prudence, cleansing.

Typewriter: Repetitive motion, unbroken cycles, habits.

Video Player: Need to review a problem or situation with close scrutiny.

Wallet: Treasures, security, family pride.

Wheel: Cycles, fate or luck. Coins are appropriate substitutes.

Whirlpool: Blending, movement, the element of Water, relaxation and healing.

Windmill: Natural energy, return to basics, element of Air.

Suggested Sources for Miscellaneous Objects

- Newspapers, magazines, and advertisements (you know, all that "junk mail" which otherwise just gets tossed out).

- Catalogs, especially from department stores or discount houses. Also, the "specials" sheet from supermarkets and drugstores.

- Old children's encyclopedias or other picture books you don't mind cutting up.

- Pictures from the boxes of various goods (this can include cereals, hardware, etc.).

Personal Notes

Runes

For a comprehensive explanation of the runes, a bit of their history, and some uses for them, I recommend purchasing either *A Practical Guide to the Runes* by Lisa Peschel (Llewellyn Publications) or *The Book of Runes* by Ralph Blum (Oracle Books).

With regard to your personal oracle, the runes may be added to almost all of the symbols listed herein to augment your intended meaning even further, or may be employed very effectively by themselves on a wood, stone, or shell base to be cast for a reading.

Rune Symbol	Rune Name	Basic Meaning
ᛗ	Mannaz	The self, individuality
ᚷ	Gebo	Alliance, presents
ᚠ	Ansuz	Harbinger, signs
ᛟ	Othila	Isolation, sanctuary
ᚢ	Uruz	Vitality, transformation
ᛈ	Perth	Beginnings, hidden truth
ᚾ	Nauthiz	Essentials, limitation

Rune Symbol	Rune Name	Basic Meaning
□	Inguz	Productivity, initiation
⅃	Eihwaz	Protection, forethought
Y	Algiz	Safety, sentiments
⼽	Fehu	Belongings, fulfillment
ᚹ	Wunjo	Bliss, accuracy
⟨⟩	Jera	Reaping, fruitfulness
⟨	Kano	Entrance, clear meaning
↑	Teiwaz	The warrior force
ᛒ	Berkana	Development, rebirth
ᛘ	Ehwaz	Activity, headway
ᚱ	Laguz	Flow, emotional needs
ᚺ	Hagalaz	Disorder, awakening
ᚱ	Raido	Travel, communication
ᚦ	Thurisaz	Gateway, standstill
ⵌ	Dagaz	Metamorphosis, day
I	Isa	Deadlock, ice
⚡	Sowelu	Completeness, life force
(Blank)		Unknowable, the Void

Personal Notes

Summary

As you can see, the lists in this chapter represent only a small fraction of all the symbols we could use for personalized oracles. The idea behind even trying to assemble such as list is to help you discover among the thousands of images you could use, those few which really provide a deep personal reaction. This response, when properly directed, helps you not only create a divination tool, but understand the mystery of life better.

If you are interested in exploring symbolism more, just take a close look at the world around you. You do not need hundreds of publications to see what is right before your eyes: the potential for inventive, timeless magic every day.

APPENDIX A

Types of Divination

For I dipt into the future, far as human eye could see,
Saw the Vision of the world,
and all the wonder that would be ...

Alfred, Lord Tennyson

Aeromancy: Observing atmospheric phenomena.

Alectromancy: Determining the future by observing roosters picking up grain.

Alphitomancy: Swallowing of a specially baked barley loaf to see if a person is guilty of lying.

Axinomancy: Divining "yes" or "no" questions by observing a stone balanced on a red hot axe.

Bibliomancy: Determining the answer to a question from random choice readings in books.

Botanomancy: Observing burning briar or vervain branches.

Capnomancy: Watching the patterns in smoke to ascertain the answer to various questions.

Carromancy: See ceromancy.

Catoptromancy: Scrying by mirror.

Cephalomancy: Divination by boiling a donkey's head.

Ceromancy: Examination of shapes when wax is dripped into water.

Chalcomancy: Interpreting the tones of copper or brass bowls when struck randomly.

Chresmomancy: Explaining the utterances of a person suffering a seizure.

Cromniomancy: Observation of growth in specially prepared onions.

Dactylomancy: Determining various personality traits by fingers and/or rings.

Daphnomancy: Prophesy by the sound of burning laurel leaves.

Felidomancy: Predictions through the behavior and action of cats.

Floromancy: Study and interpretation of the significance of various flowers and plants.

Gelomancy: Representations of hysterical laughter.

Geomancy: Divination by markings on the earth, or by soil.

Gyromancy: Medium-translated mutterings of those exhausted by ecstatic dance.

Halomancy: Visions by casting salt into fire and observing both the flame and sounds made.

Hippomancy: Reviewing the gait of horses during ceremonial processions.

Hydromancy: Any divinations which use water as an elemental component.

Ichthyomancy: Examination of live or dead fish.

Lithomancy: Reflection of candlelight in precious stones.

Lychnomancy: Watching flames of three candles forming a triangle.

Macharomancy: Swords, daggers, and knives.

Margaritomancy: Actions of a charmed pearl in a covered pot.

Metopomancy: Lines on a person's forehead.

Metoposcopy: See metopomancy.

Myomancy: Sounds and actions of suddenly appearing mice.

Nephelomancy: Movement and shape of clouds.

Oenomancy: Color, appearance, and taste of wines.

Omphalomancy: Contemplation of one's navel.

Oneiromancy: Dreams and night visions.

Onomatomancy: Names.

Onychomancy: Reflection of sunlight on fingernails.

Ophiomancy: Study of serpents.

Ornithomancy: Divination by birds.

Ovomancy: Observing shapes formed by egg whites in water.

Phyllorhodomancy: Sounds of rose leaves clapped against the hand.

Podomancy: Soles of the feet.

Psychomancy: Gazing into people's souls.

Pyromancy: Gazing into fire.

Rhabdomancy: Use of divining rods.

Scapulomancy: Markings on the shoulder bone of animals.

Sciomancy: Size, shape, and changing appearances of shadows.

Selenomancy: Phases and appearance of the moon.

Sideromancy: Shapes formed by dropping dry straw on hot iron.

Splanchomancy: Entrails of sacrificial animals.

Spodomancy: Patterns left in ashes.

Sycomancy: Drying of fig leaves.

Transataumancy: Events seen or heard accidentally.

Tyromancy: Coagulation of cheese.

Uromancy: Inspection of urine.

Xylomancy: Appearance of fallen tree branches, or position of burning logs, randomly thrown sticks, or straw.

Zoomancy: Reports of imaginary beasts such as the Loch Ness monster.

APPENDIX B

Expressing Sentiments

This is the state of man: to-day he puts forth
The tender leaves of hope; to-morrow blossoms,
And bears his blushing honours thick upon him ...

William Shakespeare

It was a favorite pastime of Victorians to give a single flower or entire nosegay of flowers, herbs, and vines to communicate specific feelings, especially those of a romantic nature. If you would like to follow in the footsteps of our ancestors by trying to create such thematic arrangements for your altar, sacred space, etc., or use the language of flowers further for your magic (such as with incense or oils), I certainly encourage you to do so. For example, if you want to create an appropriate arrangement for your altar when you are doing a ritual for prosperity, allspice, beech, and wheat would all be suitable. Good choices in doing a spell for a friend are zinnia and fern.

Other ways to use the language of flowers include reversing the plant in the arrangement to likewise reverse the energy, such as turning a dead leaf upside-down to help bring an end to sadness. This particular example also has the symbolic advantage of "turning over a new leaf." Another application might be to crush, burn, or bury the chosen item to signify and give power to change. For instance, if working magic to stop gossip, you might burn hop as part of the incense to burn away injustice.

Within the space of this book I could not cover all the plants included in the numerous lists of flower language. In order to augment your magical efforts, here is an abbreviated list of plants not already listed in this book.

Broken Straw: Dissension, conflict.

Acacia: Elegance, grace, refinement.

Allspice: Benevolence, charity, helpfulness.

Amaryllis: Pride, dignity.

Azalea: Temperance, prudence, moderation.

Bachelor's-button: Hope in love.

Beech: Prosperity, financial stability.

Belladonna: Imagination, creativity.

Bramble: Envy, rivalry.

Currant: Pleasantries, joy, good will.

Cabbage: Profits, improved money flow, good investment.

Cactus: Burning desire, zealousness.

Coriander: Hidden talents or spiritual gifts.

Dahlia: Instability, weakness.

Dead Leaf: Melancholy, sadness.

Endive: Conservative actions, frugality, caution.

Fern: Sincerity, honesty, candor.

Flax: Domestic labors, care of home.

Garland of Roses: Reward of excellence.

Grass: Utility, usefulness, practicality.

Holly: Foresight, planning, wisdom.

Hop: Prejudice, injustice.

Jonquil: Affections returned equally.

Lady's-slipper: Fickleness, frivolity, changeableness.

Lemon: Zest, energy, vitality.

Magnolia: Love of nature, any work with the land.

Mimosa: Sensitivity, empathy, understanding.

Mullein: Good-naturedness.

Mushroom: Suspicion, hunches.

Narcissus: Ego, pride.

Oxeye: Tolerance, patience, perseverance.

Periwinkle: Good memories, joyous occasions.

Pineapple: Perfection, quality.

Potato: Charity, kindness.

Quince: Temptation, fascination, desire.

Reed: Music, harmony.

Rue: Purification, cleansing.

Rush: Peacefulness, contentment.

Shamrock: Joy, happiness, pleasure.

Snowdrop: Hope, faith, opportunity.

Sweet William: Honor, gallantry, chivalry.

Thorn: Security, safety.

Trefoil: Unity, wholeness, accord.

Truffle: Astonishment, surprises, wonder.

Turnip: Benevolence, service, charity.

Valerian: Accommodation, hospitality, rest.

Watermelon: Bulkiness, anything cumbersome.

Wheat: Riches, prosperity, the promise of plenty.

Wormwood: Scarcity, absence.

Zinnia: Friendship, kinship, family ties.

BIBLIOGRAPHY

Beyerl, Paul. *The Master Book of Herbalism.* Custer, WA: Phoenix Publishing, 1984.

Black, William G. *Folk-Medicine: A Chapter in the History of Culture.* New York, NY: Burt Franklin Publishing, 1970. (Repr. of 1883 ed.)

Blackerby, M. *Cosmic Keys.* St. Paul, MN: Llewellyn Publications, 1991.

Bramson, Ann. *Soap: Making It, Enjoying It.* New York, NY: Workman Publishing Co., 1972.

Bravo, Brett. *Healing with Crystals.* New York, NY: Warner Books, 1988.

Buckland, Raymond. *Practical Color Magick.* St. Paul, MN: Llewellyn Publications, 1985.

Budge, E.A. Wallis. *Amulets and Superstitions.* New York, NY: Dover Publications, 1978.

Campanelli, Pauline. *Ancient Ways.* St. Paul, MN: Llewellyn Publications, 1991.

Cavendish, Richard. *A History of Magic.* New York, NY: Taplinger Publishing, 1977.

Chardenon, Ludo. *In Praise of Wild Herbs.* Santa Barbara, CA: Capra Press, 1975.

Chase, A.W., M.D. and F.B. Dickenson. *Dr. Chase's Last Complete Work.* 1908.

Chaundler, Christine. *The Book of Superstitions.* New York, NY: Citadel Press, 1970.

Clifton, Claire. *Edible Flowers*. New York, NY: McGraw-Hill Publishing, 1976.

Cristiani, R.S. *Perfumery and Kindred Arts*. PA: Baird & Co, 1877.

Cross, Jean. *In Grandmother's Day*. Englewood Cliffs, NJ: Prentice Hall, 1980.

Culpeper, Nicholas. *Culpeper's Complete Herbal and English Physician*. Glenwood, IL: Meyerbooks, 1987. (Repr. of 1814 ed.)

_____ . *Culpeper's Herbal Remedies*. North Hollywood, CA: Wilshire Book Co, 1979.

Cunningham, Scott. *The Magic in Food*. St. Paul, MN: Llewellyn Publications, 1991.

_____ . *The Magic of Incense, Oils & Brews*. St. Paul, MN: Llewellyn Publications, 1982.

_____ . *Magical Herbalism*. St. Paul, MN: Llewellyn Publications, 1983.

Edmonds, I.G. *Second Sight*. NY: Thomas Nelson Publishers, 1977.

Evaine, Lady Arwen. *The Complete Anachronisms Guide to Brewing*. CA: SCA Inc., 1990.

Evans, Susan. *Pomanders and Sweetbags*. NY: Falconwood Press, 1988.

Fox, William, M.D. *The Model Botanic Guide to Health*. White & Son Publishing Co., 1907.

Gayre, R. *Brewing Mead*. Boulder, CO: Brewers Publications, 1986.

Gordon, L. *Green Magic*. New York, NY: Viking, 1977.

Green, Stephanie. *Flower Power*. NY: Merimac Co.

Hall, Manly P. *The Secret Teachings of All Ages*. Los Angeles, CA: Philosophical Research Society, 1978.

Hobson, Phyllis. *Making Wines, Beers, and Soft Drinks*. Pownal, VT: Garden Way Publishing, 1976.

Innes, Brian. *The Tarot: How to Use and Interpret the Cards.* NY: Crescent Books, 1976.

Kieckhefer, Richard. *Magic in the Middle Ages.* New York, NY: Cambridge University Press, 1990.

Kunz, George F. *Curious Lore of Precious Stones.* New York, NY: Dover Publications, 1970.

Leighton, Ann. *American Gardens in the Nineteenth Century.* Amherst, MA: University of Massachusetts Press, 1987.

MacNicol, Mary. *The Art of Flower Cooking.* New York, NY: Fleet Press, 1967.

Man, Myth and Magic: The Illustrated Encyclopedia of Mythology, Religion and the Unknown. 2nd ed. Ed. by Richard Cavendish. Freeport, NY: Marshall Cavendish, 1983.

Mercatante, A. *The Magic Garden.* New York, NY: Harper & Row, 1976.

_____ . *Zoo of the Gods.* New York, NY: Harper & Row, 1974.

Mohr, Merilyn. *The Art of Soap Making.* Buffalo, NY: Firefly Books, 1979.

Northcote, Lady Rosaline. *The Book of Herb Lore.* New York, NY: Dover Publications, 1912.

Oracles and Divination. Ed. by Michael Loewe and Carmen Blacker. Boston, MA: Shambhala Publications, 1981.

Palaiseul, Jean. *Grandmother's Secrets.* New York, NY: G.P. Putnam's Sons, 1973.

Plat, Sir Hugh. *Delights for Ladies.* NY: Falconwood Press, 1988.

Riotte, Louise. *Sleeping with a Sunflower.* Pownal, VT: Garden Way Publishing, 1987.

Rodale's Illustrated Encyclopedia of Herbs. Ed. by Rodale Books editors and William H. Hylton. Emmaus, PA: Rodale Press, 1987.

Rohde, Eleanour S. *Olde English Herbals.* New York, NY: Dover Publications, 1989.

Rose, Jeanne. *Kitchen Cosmetics: Using Plants and Herbs in Cosmetics.* North Hollywood, CA: Panjandrum Books, 1978.

Sams, Jamie and David Carson. *Medicine Cards: The Discovery of Power Through the Ways of Animals.* Santa Fe, NM: Bear & Company, 1988.

Sanecki, Kay N. *The Book of Herbs.* Secaucus, NJ: Book Sales, Inc., 1987.

Schapira, Joel, David, and Karl. *The Book of Coffee and Tea.* New York, NY: St. Martin's Press, 1982.

Scourse, Nicollette. *The Victorians and Their Flowers.* Portland, OR: Timber Press, 1983.

Shaudys, Phyllis V. *Herbal Treasures.* Pownal, VT: Garden Way Publishing, 1990.

Singer, C. *From Magic to Science.* New York, NY: Dover Publications, 1958.

Summer Rain, Mary. *Earthway.* New York, NY: Pocket Books, 1990.

Swarthout, Doris L. *An Age of Flowers-Nature: Sense and Sentiment in Victorian America.* Greenwich, CT: Chatham Press, 1975.

Thomas, Mai. *Granny's Remedies.* New York, NY: James H. Heineman, Inc., 1965.

Tillona, P. *Feast of Flowers.* New York, NY: Funk & Wagnalls Co., 1969.

Visions and Prophecies. (Mysteries of the Unknown Series.) Alexandria, VA: Time-Life Books, 1988.

Weed, Susun S. *Healing Wise.* NY: Ash Tree Publishing, 1989.

Whiteside, Robert L. *Animal Language.* NY: Frederick Fell Publishing, 1981.

Wootton, A. *Animal Folklore, Myth and Legend.* New York, NY: Blandford Press, 1986.

INDEX

G

H

M

N

Stay in Touch

On the following pages you will find listed, with their current prices, some of the books now available on related subjects. Your book dealer stocks most of these and will stock new titles in the Llewellyn series as they become available. We urge your patronage.

To obtain our full catalog, to keep informed about new titles as they are released and to benefit from informative articles and helpful news, you are invited to write for our bimonthly news magazine/catalog, *Llewellyn's New Worlds of Mind and Spirit*. A sample copy is free, and it will continue coming to you at no cost as long as you are an active mail customer. Or you may subscribe for just $10.00 in the U.S.A. and Canada ($20.00 overseas, first class mail). Many bookstores also have *New Worlds* available to their customers. Ask for it.

Stay in touch! In *New Worlds'* pages you will find news and features about new books, tapes and services, announcements of meetings and seminars, articles helpful to our readers, news of authors, products and services, special money-making opportunities, and much more.

Llewellyn's New Worlds of Mind and Spirit
P.O. Box 64383-786, St. Paul, MN 55164-0383, U.S.A.

* * *

To Order Books and Tapes

If your book dealer does not have the books described on the following page readily available, you may order them directly from the publisher by sending full price in U.S. funds, plus $3.00 for postage and handling for orders under $10.00; $4.00 for orders over $10.00. There are no postage and handling charges for orders over $50.00. Postage and handling rates are subject to change. UPS Delivery: We ship UPS whenever possible. Delivery guaranteed. Provide your street address as UPS does not deliver to P.O. Boxes. Allow 4-6 weeks for delivery. UPS to Canada requires a $50.00 minimum order. Orders outside the U.S.A. and Canada: airmail—add retail price of book; add $5.00 for each non-book item (tapes, etc.); add $1.00 per item for surface mail.

For Group Study and Purchase

Because there is a great deal of interest in group discussion and study of the subject matter of this book, we feel that we should encourage the adoption and use of this particular book by such groups by offering a special quantity price to group leaders or agents. Our special quantity price for a minimum order of five copies of *The Victorian Flower Oracle* is $38.85 cash-with-order. This price includes postage and handling within the United States. Minnesota residents must add 6.5% sales tax. For additional quantities, please order in multiples of five. For Canadian and foreign orders, add postage and handling charges as above. Credit card (VISA, MasterCard, American Express) orders are accepted. Charge card orders only ($15.00 minimum order) may be phoned in free within the U.S.A. or Canada by dialing 1-800-THE-MOON. For customer service, call 1-612-291-1970. Mail orders to:

LLEWELLYN PUBLICATIONS
P.O. Box 64383-786, St. Paul, MN 55164-0383, U.S.A.

A VICTORIAN GRIMOIRE
by Patricia Telesco

Like a special opportunity to rummage through your grandmother's attic, *A Victorian Grimoire* offers you a personal invitation to discover a storehouse of magical treasures. Enhance every aspect of your daily life as you begin to reclaim the romance, simplicity and "know-how" of the Victorian era—that exceptional period of American history when people's lives and times were shaped by their love of the land, of home and family, and by their simple acceptance of magic as part of everyday life.

More and more, people are searching for ways to create peace and beauty in this increasingly chaotic world. This special book shows you how to recreate that peace and beauty with simple, down-to-earth "Victorian Enchantments" that turn every mundane act into an act of magic ... from doing the dishes ... to making beauty-care products ... to creating games for children. This book is a handy reference when you need a specific spell, ritual, recipe, or tincture for any purpose. What's more, *A Victorian Grimoire* is a captivating study of the turn of the century and a comprehensive repository of common-sense knowledge. Learn how to relieve a backache, dry and store herbs, help children get over fears of the dark, treat pets with first aid, and much more.

0-87542-784-7, 368 pgs., 7 x 10, illus., softcover　　　　　　　**$14.95**

THE URBAN PAGAN
Magical Living in a 9-to-5 World
by Patricia Telesco

Finally, a book that takes into account the problems of city-dwelling magicians! When preparing to do ritual, today's magician is often faced with busy city streets and a vast shortage of private natural space in which to worship. Technology surrounds, and fear and misunderstanding still exist about "magic" and "witchcraft." This leaves even experienced spiritual seekers trying desperately to carry a positive magical lifestyle into the 21st century. With the help of *The Urban Pagan*, we all can learn to incorporate Earth-aware philosophies of days gone by with modern realities.

The Urban Pagan is a transformational book of spells, rituals, herbals, invocations, and meditations that will help the reader to build inner confidence, create a magical living environment, and form an urban wheel of the year. It updates interpretations of symbolism for use in sympathetic magic and visualization, shows how to make magical tools inexpensively, provides daily magical exercises that can aid in seasonal observances, shows practical ways to help heal the Earth, and explains the art of cultivating and using herbs, plus much more.

0-87542-785-5, 336 pgs., 6 x 9, illus., softcover　　　　　　　**$13.00**

CUNNINGHAM'S ENCYCLOPEDIA OF CRYSTAL, GEM & METAL MAGIC
by Scott Cunningham

Here you will find the most complete information anywhere on the magical qualities of more than 100 crystals and gemstones as well as several metals. The information for each crystal, gem, or metal includes: its related energy, planetary rulership, magical element, deities, Tarot card, and the magical powers that each is believed to possess. Also included is a complete description of their uses for magical purposes. The classic on the subject.

0-87542-126-1, 240 pgs., 6 x 9, illus., color plates, softcover $12.95

HERB MAGIC VIDEO
with Scott Cunningham

This is the ultimate home-study course in herbalism form master herbalist Scott Cunningham. You'll learn to harvest and cure natural herbs; prepare ancient recipes for magical incense, sachets and talismans; and create pure herbal essences and tinctures. You and Scott will visit a working herb farm to learn how to identify many common and rare herbs on sight. Discover and use the power of herb magic and spells—secrets that are revealed here for the very first time. It is often easier to learn something by having it demonstrated to you than it is when you read about it in a book. With this videotape Cunningham gives you a personal lesson in herb magic!

0-87542-117-2, American VHS only, 1 hour $29.95

THE COMPLETE BOOK OF INCENSE, OILS & BREWS
by Scott Cunningham

For centuries the composition of incenses, the blending of oils, and the mixing of herbs have been used by people to create positive changes in their lives. With this book, the curtains of secrecy have been drawn back, providing you with practical, easy-to-understand information that will allow you to practice these methods of magical cookery.

Scott Cunningham, world-famous expert on magical herbalism, first published *The Magic of Incense, Oils & Brews* in 1986. *The Complete Book of Incense, Oils & Brews* is a revised and expanded version of that book. Scott took readers' suggestions from the first edition and added more than 100 new formulas. Every page has been clarified and rewritten, and new chapters have been added.

There is no special, costly equipment to buy, and ingredients are usually easy to find. The book includes detailed information on a wide variety of herbs, sources for purchasing ingredients, substitutions for hard-to-find herbs, a glossary, and a chapter on creating your own magical recipes.

0-87542-128-8, 288 pgs., 6 x 9, illus., softcover $12.95

Prices subject to change without notice.

CUNNINGHAM'S ENCYCLOPEDIA OF MAGICAL HERBS
by Scott Cunningham

This is the most comprehensive source of herbal data for magical uses ever printed! Almost every one of the over 400 herbs are illustrated, making this a great source for herb identification. For each herb you will also find: magical properties, planetary rulerships, genders, associated deities, folk and Latin names, and much more. To make this book even easier to use, it contains a folk name cross reference, and all of the herbs are fully indexed. There is also a large annotated bibliography and a list of mail order suppliers so you can find the books and herbs you need.

Like all of Cunningham's books, this one does not require you to use complicated rituals or expensive magical paraphernalia. Instead, it shares with you the intrinsic powers of the herbs. Thus, you will be able to discover which herbs, by their very nature, can be used for luck, love, success, money, divination, astral projection, safety, psychic self-defense, and much more.

Besides being interesting and educational it is also fun and fully illustrated with unusual woodcuts from old herbals. This book has rapidly become the classic in its field. It enhances books such as *777* and is a must for all Wiccans.

0-87542-122-9, 336 pgs., 6 x 9, illus., softcover   **$12.95**

THE MAGIC IN FOOD
Legends, Lore & Spells
by Scott Cunningham

Foods are storehouses of natural energies. Choosing specific foods, properly preparing them, eating with a magical goal in mind: these are the secrets of food magic, an age-old method of taking control of your life through your diet.

Though such exotic dishes as bird's-nest soup and saffron bread are included in this book, you'll find many old friends: peanut butter and jelly sandwiches … scrambled eggs … tofu … beer. We've consumed them for years, but until we're aware of the energies contained within them, foods offer little more than nourishment and pleasure.

You'll learn the mystic qualities of everyday dishes, their preparation (if any) and the simple method of calling upon their powers. The author has included numerous magical diets, each designed to create a specific change within its user: increased health and happiness, deeper spirituality, enhanced sexual relations, protection, psychic awareness, success, love, prosperity—all through the hidden powers of food.

0-87542-130-X, 384 pgs., 6 x 9, illus., color plates, softcover   **$14.95**

Prices subject to change without notice.

THE MAGICAL HOUSEHOLD
Empower Your Home with Love, Protection, Health and Happiness
by Scott Cunningham and David Harrington

Whether your home is a small apartment or a palatial mansion, you want it to be something special. Now it can be with *The Magical Household*. Learn how to make your home more than just a place to live. Turn it into a place of security, life, fun, and magic. Here you will not find the complex magic of the ceremonial magician. Rather, you will learn simple, quick, and effective magical spells that use nothing more than common items in your house: furniture, windows, doors, carpet, pets, etc. You will learn to take advantage of the intrinsic power and energy that is already in your home, waiting to be tapped. You will learn to make magic a part of your life. The result is a home that is safeguarded from harm and a place which will bring you happiness, health, and more.

0-87542-124-5, 208 pgs., 5-1/4 x 8, illus., softcover   **$8.95**

SPELL CRAFTS
Creating Magical Objects
by Scott Cunningham and David Harrington

Since early times, crafts have been intimately linked with spirituality. When a woman carefully shaped a water jar from the clay she'd gathered from a river bank, she was performing a spiritual practice. When crafts were used to create objects intended for ritual or that symbolized the Divine, the connection between the craftsperson and divinity grew more intense. Today, handcrafts can still be more than a pastime—they can be rites of power and honor; a religious ritual. After all, hands were our first magical tools.

Spell Crafts is a modern guide to creating physical objects for the attainment of specific magical goals. It is far different from magic books that explain how to use purchased magical tools. You will learn how to fashion spell brooms, weave wheat, dip candles, sculpt clay, mix herbs, bead sacred symbols, and much more, for a variety of purposes. Whatever your craft, you will experience the natural process of moving energy from within yourself (or within natural objects) to create positive change.

0-87542-185-7, 224 pgs., 5-1/4 x 8, illus., photos, softcover   **$10.00**

MAGICAL HERBALISM
The Secret Craft of the Wise
by Scott Cunningham

Certain plants are prized for the special range of energies—the vibrations or powers—they possess. *Magical Herbalism* unites the powers of plants and man to produce, and direct, change in accord with human will and desire.

This is the magic of amulets and charms, sachets and herbal pillows, incenses and scented oils, simples and infusions and anointments. It's magic as old as our knowledge of plants, an art that anyone can learn and practice, and once again enjoy as we look to the Earth to rediscover our roots and make inner connections with the world of Nature.

This is magic that is beautiful and natural—a craft of hand and mind merged with the power and glory of Nature: a special kind that does not use the medicinal powers of herbs, but rather the subtle vibrations and scents that touch the psychic centers and stir the astral field in which we live to work at the causal level behind the material world.

This is the magic of enchantment ... of word and gesture to shape the images of mind and channel the energies of the herbs. It is a magic for everyone—for the herbs are easily and readily obtained, the tools are familiar or easily made, and the technology that of home and garden. This book includes step-by-step guidance to the preparation of herbs and to their compounding in incense and oils, sachets and amulets, simples and infusions, with rituals and spells for every purpose.

0-87542-120-2, 260 pgs., 5-1/4 x 8, illus., softcover   **$7.95**

LLEWELLYN'S MAGICAL ALMANAC

This enchanting yearly guide for Pagans has become a faithful friend to magical people the world over. It's chock full of articles, usable monthly calendars, magical advice, and captivating artwork. What's more, its value lasts beyond the year—the captivating articles on a variety of magical subjects make this a long-cherished keepsake for decades to come.

288 pgs., 5-1/4 x 8, illus., softcover   **State year $7.95**

ANCIENT WAYS
Reclaiming the Pagan Tradition
by Pauline Campanelli, illustrated by Dan Campanelli

Ancient Ways is filled with magic and ritual that you can perform every day to capture the spirit of the seasons. It focuses on the celebration of the Sabbats of the Old Religion by giving you practical things to do while anticipating the Sabbat rites, and helping you harness the magical energy for weeks afterward. The wealth of seasonal rituals and charms are drawn from ancient sources but are easily performed with materials readily available.

Learn how to look into your previous lives at Yule ... at Beltane, discover the places where you are most likely to see faeries ... make special jewelry to wear for your Lammas celebrations ... for the special animals in your life, paint a charm of protection at Midsummer.

Most Pagans and Wiccans feel that the Sabbat rituals are all too brief and wish for the magic to linger on. *Ancient Ways* can help you reclaim your own traditions and heighten the feeling of magic.

0-87542-090-7, 256 pgs., 7 x 10, illus., softcover   **$12.95**

PLAYFUL MAGIC
by Janina Renee

A carefree, playful spirit appears to be the key to an enchanted existence. Light-hearted people are genuinely luckier, and all aspects of life just seem to work better for them. Expressing the playful self, which includes nourishing the "inner child," brings spiritual and emotional enrichment. Many psychological and metaphysical systems emphasize that our playful self is connected to our personal vitality, our intuition, and the unified state of mind and being that puts us in sync with the life pulse of the universe.

Playful Magic is a "how to" book that provides magical techniques for helping your life run more smoothly. It is a collection of meditations, visualizations, magical exercises, suggestions, and philosophy aimed at taking you outside of yourself and away from worries and problems. It shows you how to recover that special quality of energy that seems to be the source, the essence of life. *Playful Magic* will help you remember that magic isn't separate from the routines of daily life—it in fact permeates all existence. To integrate magic into life is not to trivialize the deeper mysteries, but to make the mystery of living more meaningful.

0-87542-678-6, 288 pgs., 6 x 9, 50 illus., softcover   **$12.95**

ANIMAL-SPEAK
The Spiritual & Magical Powers of Creatures Great & Small
by Ted Andrews

The animal world has much to teach us. Some are experts at survival and adaptation, some never get cancer, some embody strength and courage while others exude playfulness. Animals remind us of the potential we can unfold, but before we can learn from them, we must first be able to speak with them.

Now, for perhaps the first time ever, myth and fact are combined in a manner that will teach you how to speak and understand the language of the animals in your life. *Animal-Speak* helps you meet and work with animals as totems and spirits—by learning the language of their behaviors within the physical world. It provides techniques for reading signs and omens in nature so you can open to higher perceptions and even prophecy. It reveals the hidden, mythical and realistic roles of 45 animals, 60 birds, 8 insects, and 6 reptiles.

Animals will become a part of you, revealing to you the majesty and divine in all life. They will restore your childlike wonder of the world and strengthen your belief in magic, dreams and possibilities.

0-87542-028-1, 400 pgs., 7 x 10, illus., photos, softcover $16.00

THE COMPLETE BOOK OF AMULETS & TALISMANS
by Migene González-Wippler

The pentagram, Star of David, crucifix, rabbit's foot, painted pebble, or Hand of Fatima … they all provide feelings of comfort and protection, attracting good while dispelling evil.

The joy of amulets and talismans is that they can be made and used by anyone. The forces used, and the forces invoked, are all natural forces.

Spanning the world through the diverse cultures of Sumer, Babylon, Greece, Italy, India, Western Europe, and North America, González-Wippler proves that amulets and talismans are anything but mere superstition—they are part of each man's and woman's search for spiritual connection. This book presents the entire history of these tools, their geography, and shows how anyone can create amulets and talismans to empower his or her life. Loaded with hundreds of photographs, this is the ultimate reference and how-to guide for their use.

0-87542-287-X, 304 pgs., 6 x 9, photos, softcover $12.95

COSMIC KEYS
Fortunetelling for Fun and Self-Discovery
by M. Blackerby
This book invites those just starting out in the psychic mysteries to jump in and take a revealing and positive look inside themselves and the people around them! Through the hands-on application of the Cosmic Keys—Chinese astrology (combined with Sun sign astrology), numerology, palmistry, card reading and finally, the author's original Dream Key and Universal Coloring Test—readers come away with telling insights into their individual personalities and life situations. The illustrations and coloring mantra were created especially for the workbook, and readers are encouraged to color each as they move through the book, as well as record personal data found in each section.
0-87542-027-3, 200 pgs., 7 x 10, illus., softcover   **$12.95**

HEALING HERBS & HEALTH FOODS OF THE ZODIAC
by Ada Muir, introduction by Jude C. Williams, M.H.
There was a time when every doctor was also an astrologer, for a knowledge of astrology was considered essential for diagnosing and curing an illness. *Healing Herbs & Health Foods of the Zodiac* reclaims that ancient healing tradition in a combined reprinting of two Ada Muir books: *Healing Herbs of the Zodiac* and *Health and the Sun Signs: Cell Salts in Medicinal Astrology.*

The first part of this book covers the ills most often found in each zodiacal sign, along with the herbs attributed to healing those ills. For example, nosebleeds are associated with Aries, and cayenne pepper is the historical herbal treatment. More than 70 herbs are covered in all, with illustrations of each herb to aid in identification.

The second part of the book covers the special mineral or cell salt needs of each sign. Cell salts, contained in fruits and vegetables, are necessary for the healthy activity of the human body. For example, the cell salt of Libra is sodium phosphate, used to maintain the balance between acids and alkalis. It's found in celery, spinach, and figs.

In her introduction, Master Herbalist and author Jude C. Williams increases the practical use of this book by outlining the basics of harvesting herbs and preparing tinctures, salves, and teas.
0-87542-575-5, 192 pgs., mass market, illus., softcover   **$3.99**

JUDE'S HERBAL HOME REMEDIES
Natural Health, Beauty & Home-Care Secrets
by Jude C. Williams, M.H.

There's a pharmacy—in your spice cabinet! In the course of daily life we all encounter problems that can be easily remedied through the use of common herbs—headaches, dandruff, insomnia, colds, muscle aches, burns—and a host of other afflictions known to humankind. *Jude's Herbal Home Remedies* is a simple guide to self-care that will benefit beginning or experienced herbalists with its wealth of practical advice. Most of the herbs listed are easy to obtain.

Discover how cayenne pepper promotes hair growth, why cranberry juice is a good treatment for asthma attacks, how to make a potent juice to flush out fat, how to make your own deodorants and perfumes, what herbs will get fleas off your pet, how to keep cut flowers fresh longer … the remedies and hints go on and on!

This book gives you instructions for teas, salves, tinctures, tonics, poultices, along with addresses for obtaining the herbs. Dangerous and controversial herbs are also discussed.

Grab this book and a cup of herbal tea, and discover from a Master Herbalist more than 800 ways to a simpler, more natural way of life.
0-87542-869-X, 240 pgs., 6 x 9, illus., softcover   **$9.95**

PRACTICAL COLOR MAGICK
by Raymond Buckland, Ph.D.

Color magick is powerful—and safe. Here is a sourcebook for the psychic influence of color on our physical lives. It contains complete rituals and meditations for practical applications of color magick for health, success, and love. Find full instructions on how to meditate more effectively and use color to stimulate the chakras and unfold psychic abilities. Learn to use color in divination and in the making of talismans, sigils, and magick squares.

This book will teach all the powers of light and more. You'll learn new forms of expression of your innermost self, new ways of relating to others with the secret languages of light and color. Put true color back into your life with the rich spectrum of ideas and practical magical formulas from *Practical Color Magick*!
0-87542-047-8, 160 pgs., 5-1/4 x 8, illus., softcover   **$6.95**

ROBIN WOOD TAROT DECK
created and illustrated by Robin Wood
instructions by Robin Wood and Michael Short

Tap into the wisdom of your subconscious with one of the most beautiful Tarot decks on the market today! Reminiscent of the Rider-Waite deck, the Robin Wood Tarot is flavored with nature imagery and luminous energies that will enchant you and the querent. Even the novice reader will find these cards easy and enjoyable to interpret.

Radiant and rich, these cards were illustrated with a unique technique that brings out the resplendent color of the prismacolor pencils. The shining strength of this Tarot deck lies in its depiction of the Minor Arcana. Unlike other Minor Arcana decks, this one springs to pulsating life. The cards are printed on quality card stock and boxed complete with instruction booklet, which provides the upright and reversed meanings of each card, as well as three basic card layouts. Beautiful and brilliant, the Robin Wood Tarot is a must-have deck!

0-87542-894-0, boxed set: 78-cards with booklet   **$19.95**

LLEWELLYN'S ORGANIC GARDENING ALMANAC

Get a head start in all your growing endeavors with the *Organic Gardening Almanac*. Here are leading-edge organic techniques that you can use to have a more healthy and bountiful year. Experts from the farming, gardening and landscaping fields have joined together to present views, methods, and interesting personal experiences for gardeners, farmers, homesteaders, and anyone interested in gardening or environmental issues.

For more than 90 years, thousands of *Llewellyn Moon Sign Book* users have attested to the amazing success of lunar gardening. In response to their requests we have combined the best of ancient lunar timing methods with modern organic techniques to give you exciting and new alternative approaches to simplify your "growing" needs.

Llewellyn's Organic Gardening Almanac is the only almanac to feature new and imaginative ways for Earth lovers to directly participate in the healing of the planet. Gardening by the moon makes vegetables more healthy, fruits more bountiful, and crops more vigorous. Lunar organic gardening improves our ailing environment and helps maintain economic stability. There is no other gardening guide quite like this on the market. Start your super garden off right—use the Moon and organics for your best harvest yet—the all-natural way!

0-87542-914-9, 288 pgs., 5-1/4 x 8, illus., softcover   **State year $5.95**

THE POWER OF THE RUNES
A Complete Kit for Divination & Magic
by Donald Tyson

This kit contains *Rune Magic*, Tyson's highly acclaimed guide to effective runework. In this book he clears away misconceptions surrounding this magical alphabet of the Northern Europeans, provides information on the Gods and Goddesses of the runes, and gives the meanings and uses of all 33 extant runes. The reader will be involved with practical runic rituals and will find advice on talisman, amulet, and sigil use.

This kit also includes the Rune Magic Deck. This set of 24 large cards illustrates each of the Futhark runes in a stunning 2-color format.

In addition, there is a set of four wooden rune dice in their own cloth bag. These square dice were designed by Donald Tyson himself. The user casts them down, then interprets their meanings as they appear before him. With the 24 Futhark runes graphically etched on their sides, these dice let the user perform an accurate reading in mere seconds.

0-87542-828-2, boxed set: *Rune Magic*, **24-card deck, 4 dice w/bag $24.95**

A PRACTICAL GUIDE TO THE RUNES
Their Uses in Divination and Magick
by Lisa Peschel

At last the world has a beginner's book on the Nordic runes that is written in straightforward and clear language. Each of the 25 runes is elucidated through no-nonsense descriptions and clean graphics. A rune's altered meaning in relation to other runes and its reversed position is also included. The construction of runes and accessories covers such factors as the type of wood to be used, the size of the runes, and the coloration, carving, and charging of the runes. With this book, the runes can be used in magick to effect desired results. Talismans carved with runescripts or bindrunes allow you to carry your magick in a tangible form, providing foci for your will. Four rune layouts complete with diagrams are presented with examples of specific questions to ask when consulting the runes. Rather than simple fortunetelling devices, the runes are oracular, empowered with the forces of Nature. They present information for you to make choices in your life.

0-87542-593-3, 192 pgs., mass market, illus., softcover   **$3.95**